Introduction to Business Start-Up

A Step-by-Step Guide to Successful Business Development-
Beginner Level.

10/27/2023

TABLE OF
CONTENTS

❖ Introduction
- ***Defining business ownership:*** *What it means to own a business*
- *Legal and financial responsibilities of business owners*
- *The benefits and challenges of business ownership*
- *How to establish ownership of a business*
- *Tips for successful business ownership*
- *The role and significance of business ownership in the economy*
- *The profit motivation*
- *Losses in business*
- *Different types of business ownership structures*

❖ Types of Business Ownership
- ➢ *Sole-proprietor*
- ▪ *advantages of sole-proprietorship*
- ▪ *disadvantages of sole-proprietorship*
- ▪ *registration of business name*
- ▪ *converting a sole-proprietorship into a partnership business*

- ➢ ***Business partnership firms***
- ▪ *reasons for forming a partnership*
- ▪ *sources of capital*
- ▪ *division of profits*
- ▪ *liability for losses*
- ▪ *advantages of partnership*
- ▪ *disadvantages of partnership*
- ▪ *registration of a partnership firm*

- ➢ ***Limited liability companies***
- ▪ *capital*
- ▪ *shares*
- ▪ *shareholders*
- ▪ *advantages of limited liability*

➢ **Corporation**

- *Private Companies*
- *Formation and Incorporation*
- *Share held by proxy*
- *Staying in control*
- *Unseen problems of the lack of control*
- *Franchises*
- *How franchise works*
- *Your decision*
- *Trading license*

❖ **Introduction: Production**

Types of Businesses
- ✓ **Industrial**
- • *extractive industry*
- • *processing industry*
- • *manufacturing industry*
- • *construction industry*

❖ **Commercial**
- • *Trading and Distribution*
  - ➢ **domestic trade**
    - • *retail*
    - • *large-scale store*
    - • *wholesale*

  - ➢ **International trade**
    - • *export*
    - • *import*
    - • *entréport*

❖ *Services Providing*
- • *accountancy*
- • *accommodation and catering*
- • *banking and finance*
- • *insurance*
- • *maintenance and repair*
- • *transportation*
- • *warehousing*

❖ **Consumers and Corporate Buyers**
- • *Consumers*
- • *Corporate*

❖ **Nature of Products**
- • *Necessities and Luxuries*
- • *Choice factor*

- *Essentials and Nonessentials*
- *Competition*
- *Classes of Customers*

❖ **Where to Locate a Business**
- *working from home*
- *passing trade*
- *quieter areas*
- *city outskirts*
- *Practice Examples D: Natures of Products*
- *Practical Examples E: Classes of Customers*

❖ **High Priced Products versus Low Priced Products**
- *availability of Business Premises and the Cost of Rental or Buy*

Research

❖ Introduction:

➢ *Process of Acquiring an Established Business*

✓ **Some Business Terms**

- *assets*
- *debtors*
- *liabilities*
- *creditors*
- *credit*
- *stock (inventory)*
- *accounts*

✓ **Why the Business is 'For Sale'**

- *its 'accounts'*
- *getting the real 'facts'*
- *the 'asking price' of the business*
- *the make-up of the value of a business*
- *values of assets and liabilities*
- *special 'attributes'*
- *goodwill*
- *how the price is to be paid*
- *assistance offered*
- *avoiding competition*
- *the sale agreement*

✓ **Buying Into a Partnership**

- *buying out an existing partner*
- *buying into an expanded partnership*

✓ **The Business Premises**

- *if the premises is included in the purchase price*
- *rented or leased premises*

- ✓ **The Lease**

- • **matters to look at in the lease:**

  - ✓ *area*
  - ✓ *property space*
  - ✓ *rent*
  - ✓ *dates*
  - ✓ *renewal*
  - ✓ *change of tenant*
  - ✓ *rent reviews or revisions*
  - ✓ *other payments over and above the rent.*
  - ✓ *do always make sure that:*

- ✓ **Share Holdings and Share Transfers:**

  - • *practical examples E*
  - • *practical example F*

- ➢ ***The Board of Directors:***

  - • *executive and non-executive directors*
  - • *company officials*
  - • *directors' fees*
  - • *dividends*
  - • *statutory obligations*

Chapter 5 – Furnishing and Equipping the Business Premises

Introduction:

➢ *Factors which dictate needs of the businesses*

✓ **Layout of the premises:**

- *planning the layout*
- *multi-room and*
- *open plan layout*

✓ **Regulations and Fittings:**
- *electrical fittings*
- *plug sockets and lighting*

➢ **Telephones:**
- *installation and connection*
➢ **Computers:**
- *siting, electrics, network cabling*
- **Walls and ceilings:**
- *painting, colors*
- *floor coverings*
- *carpeting and other materials*
- *heating and/or cooling*
- *furniture*
- *counters*
✓ **Machinery & Equipment:**
- *hiring, renting or leasing, hire purchasing*
➢ **Working Assets:**
- *depreciation – wear and tear*
➢ **Doors and Windows:**
- *security*
- *the outside*
- *signs – licenses to erect*
✓ **Window Displays:**
- *attracting favorable attention*
- *designing and creating*
- *planning*

- *building*
- *keeping attraction*
- *displays for services*
- *internal displays*
- *safety consideration*
- *security against shoplifting*
- ✓ **Insurance:**
- *what is involved?*
- *risks faced*
- *indemnity*
- *risk against which businesses may insure*
- *insurance needed*
- *why some risk are not insured against*
- *loss of profits insurance*
- *reducing risks*

Practical Example: F

Introduction
➢ **Wholesaler Businesses: Streamlining Supply Chains for Efficiency and Profitability**

- *wholesale business*
- *retail business*
- *groups of wholesalers and retailers*
- *buying or purchasing*
- *orders and ordering*
- *finding suppliers*
- *catalogues and price list*
- *quotation and estimates*
- *choosing suppliers*

Practical Example: G

✓ **Order Forms:**
- *receiving deliveries*
- *storage of stock*
- *why stores are needed*
- *costs of storage*
- *location of stores*
- *stores doorways and other opening*
- *stores floors*
- *heating/cooling in stores*
- *stores layout*
- *stores equipment*

✓ **Stock Control:**
- *prevention of theft*
- *prevention of Pilfering*
- *protection of items in the store*
- *fire precautions*

✓ **Stock Records:**

- *basic stock records*
- *accuracy in stock records*
- *stock levels*
- *setting the correct stock levels*
- *stocktaking and spot checks*

Chapter 1
THE FIRST STEPS

What is a Business?

Starting a business can be an exciting and rewarding venture, but it can also be overwhelming and confusing, especially if you are new to the world of entrepreneurship. Before you dive into the world of business start-ups, it is important to have a clear understanding of what exactly a business is and what it entails. In this chapter, we will provide an introduction to business start-up and answer questions such as "What is a business?" and "What are the key elements of a successful business?" Whether you are considering starting your own business or simply curious about the fundamentals of business ownership, this chapter will provide you with a solid foundation to build upon. So let's get started and gain a comprehensive understanding of what it takes to start and run a successful business.

Legal and financial responsibilities of business owners

As a business owner, it is crucial to understand the legal and financial responsibilities that come with each ownership structure. The legal and financial obligations can vary significantly depending on the type of business structure you choose. Let's take a closer look at the responsibilities associated with each ownership structure:

1. **Sole proprietorships:** As the sole owner of the business, you have complete control over the decision-making process. However, it is important to note that you are personally liable for all the debts and obligations of the business. This means that if the business fails to repay its debts, your personal assets may be at risk.

2. **Partnerships:** In a partnership, all partners share the responsibility for the business's debts and legal obligations. It is essential to have a well-

drafted partnership agreement that outlines the rights, responsibilities, and profit-sharing arrangements among partners.

3. **Limited Liability Companies (LLCs):** One of the significant advantages of an LLC is that it offers limited liability protection to its members. This means that members' personal assets are usually protected from the company's debts and legal obligations. However, it is essential to adhere to all the legal requirements for forming and maintaining an LLC to enjoy this liability protection.

4. **Corporations:** As a shareholder of a corporation, your liability is typically limited to the amount you have invested in the company. However, corporations have more complex legal and financial responsibilities. They are required to follow strict corporate governance, maintain proper records, and comply with various reporting and tax obligations.

Understanding the legal and financial responsibilities of each ownership structure is essential for making an informed decision that aligns with your business goals and personal circumstances. Consulting with legal and financial professionals can provide valuable guidance in navigating these responsibilities.

What are Products?

When starting a business, it is essential to have a clear understanding of the products you will be offering. Products can encompass a wide range of offerings, including goods, and services. By understanding the different types of products and how they fit into your business model, you can better position your start-up for success. The range of products available for sale and purchase today can be of great importance in many countries; in this Chapter, we will provide an introduction to the concept of products and explore the various categories they fall under. Whether you are launching a physical product or a service-based business, this information will be invaluable as you navigate the world of entrepreneurship.

The products are only of two distinct types:-

❖ **Goods**

What we call 'goods' are items which can be seen and touched, and many of them can be smelt or tasted or heard; we say that they are 'tangible' or 'physical' items. Items of goods range from food and drinks to clothes, footwear and medicines; from simple items like pins and paperclips and books, to computers, motor vehicles, aeroplanes, satellites and space vehicles; from doorknobs to bridges and oil refineries. The list is endless, and is continually being added to!

There are some items called 'staple products; which are mainly important or essential foodstuffs; such as rice in many countries, maize in others, flour or yams in others, and so on. Many people in the countries cannot live or survive without these products; they are sometimes called 'necessities'.

Some people in business make or 'manufacture' goods; they might be tailors or bakers or furniture-makers, for example; they might work in small workshops; or they might manufacture their goods in factories. They are often called 'manufacturers'. Other people in business grow crops or raise cattle, for example as farmers or ranchers; they are often called 'producers'.

Business people who do not make or produce goods, but who buy and sell them are said to be in 'distribution', they are called 'distributors'.

Different types of goods might be called by different names, such as 'produce' (mainly agricultural – farm or dairy products), "materials", "supplies", "trade goods". "stock" or ' inventory", and so on. The products used in making another product are called 'components'. For example, to build a wall a builder needs bricks, cement and sand. To make a chair a carpenter needs wood (timber), nails, screws, glue, and so on.

❖ Services

Other products are 'intangible', that is they cannot be seen or felt. They usually involve some kind of work, only the 'results' of which can be seen or felt. For example, a mechanic who repairs a broken machine has performed a service; the machine now operates – when previously it did not.

Services are performed by people in many other occupations, such as builders, carpenters, painters and decorators, hairdressers, tailors, waiters, gardeners, windows cleaners, salespeople, managers, bookkeepers, secretaries, restauranteurs, hoteliers, estate agents, travel agents, and many more.
It is a little confusing that some service-providers, like electricians, carpenters, painters and decorators, are called 'tradesmen', when they are not in trade.

The Idea for your business

Finding the perfect idea for your business can be a daunting task. With countless options and the pressure to create something innovative and successful, it's easy to feel overwhelmed. But fear not – this Chapter is here to help guide you through the process of generating and evaluating business ideas. Whether you're a seasoned entrepreneur or a first-time business owner, this Chapter will provide you with practical tips and strategies to help you find the ideal business idea that aligns with your passions and has the potential for profitability. So, let's dive in and discover the key steps to turning your business idea into a reality.

You might have found a product to manufacture, or an idea for one. Or perhaps you have decided to go into distribution, or to provide a service. It is important that you know what you want to do – what your 'goal' is. Only you can make the decision on your choice of business "venture". After all, you are in the best position to know where your interest lie, what skills and abilities and capabilities you have, and which of them form the best foundation for your new 'career' in business.

You might feel able to make use of skills or knowledge of a trade or profession, or business training or sales/managerial experience you have gained in previous work. But if you have been unhappy or have felt unfulfilled in your previous work, you might want to "strike out" in a new direction; a new 'venture'.

Perhaps a hobby has gained you proficiency in some field – for example, cooking or dressmaking or gardening or woodworking – which can be the beginnings of a business. You might have formed the basis of a customer or client-list, and have gained an idea of the potential "market". If you have also gained money "income" from your spare-time activities, that, too, can help greatly, as you will definitely need some money with which to start or take over a business.

You might have designed or invented a new product which fills a "gap" in the market, which nobody else has noticed. You will need to be sure there will be a 'demand'; that is, people will buy and pay for the product. Or you might have an idea for a new or improved service, which people or other businesses will find useful or beneficial and will pay for.

You might want to enter an established type of business or trade, perhaps by buying or taking over a existing business, or by buying a franchise, or buying into a partnership. If the type or 'line' of business or trade is new to you – be wary. You might find it very difficult to master it at the same time as learning how to run a business. You will be competing with others who are already experienced, and who might be experts, in that particular line of business or trade. It is safer to gain some experience by working in a similar business or trade first, and by understanding training, like this program.

It is usually best to avoid starting or taking over a business which is dependent on the skills of another person or more than one rather than on your own skills. You could face serious difficulties if a person on whom you depend were to "let you down", or fail to perform to your expectations, or leaves to work elsewhere.

Another matter you need to realize early on is that, as a business owner, you will probably have to work hard and perhaps for longer hours (maybe even over weekends and public holidays) than you might have to work or have had to work as an employee for somebody else. As a business owner, it might be more difficult for you to have "time off" or to take paid holidays. To become a successful business person you need commitment, as well as the willingness to work hard and long hours.

The Business Plan

A business plan is an essential document for any entrepreneur or business owner. It serves as a roadmap for success, outlining the goals, strategies, and financial projections of a company. A well-crafted business plan not only helps secure funding and attract investors, but also provides a clear direction for the business and ensures that all stakeholders are aligned.

Whether you are starting a new venture or looking to grow an existing one, understanding the key components of a business plan is crucial. In this Chapter, we will explore the fundamentals of a business plan and provide valuable tips for creating a comprehensive and effective document. Read on to discover the power of a well-designed business plan and how it can drive your success in the highly competitive business world.

Because there are so many kinds and sizes of businesses, engaged in so many different types of activities, there is no set format for a Business Plan. However, we can give you general guidelines of what needs to be included in most **instances:-**

❖   What the **activities of the business will be**:

> *Is it going to make or produce products – if so what?*
> *Is it going to buy and sell products – if so what?*
> *Is it going to provide a service – if so what?*

In other words, the "nature" or substance of the business has to be made clear.

❖ What **activities the business will be involved in to achieve its objectives;**
what actions will have to be taken, and in what manner those activities will be carried out or performed, For example, if the business is going to be involved in trading, the plan will have to show how and from whom goods will be bought, to whom and by what method of selling the goods will be used.

❖ **Who will run the business**, and/or work in it. The owner of the business might work alone, or have family-members to assist, or have to employ one or more employees, or work with a "partner". The experience, training, knowledge and skills of the owners/partners should be listed.

❖ **From where the business will operate**, its premises: from a shop or store, office, workshop or factory – even, perhaps, to begin with from home.

❖ What **'market'** there is for the products the business is going to make, produce, buy and sell or provide? By this we mean, who its customers or clients will be, and how many there are likely to be who are willing and able (who can afford) to pay for its products.

❖ **What competitors there are**; that is, other businesses making or producing or buying and selling or providing the same or similar products, especially in the area, or "locally" or "vicinity".

❖ A **'funds forecast'** dealing with financial matters. These include how much money is needed to start the business; to buy machinery and equipment; to buy stocks of goods or materials or components; to rent or buy premises; to pay expenses, to attract customers, and to keep the business "running" until it earns income from its activities. Also, how much, if any money is ready available, how much will have to be "raised" from other sources, and what those sources are likely to be. We deal with these very important topics in the next Section, under the heading **'Capital'**.

❖   A **'profits forecast**; that is, an indication of how much profit the business can realistically be expected to gain, year by year for, say, three years ahead. The owner (s) of the business will have to "estimate" (to calculate roughly, but as accurately as possible) the amounts of income they expect the business to receive and the amounts of expenditure to be paid out, year by year.

You will expect to be "paid"- to receive an "income" – for all the hard work you will have to "put into", or "invest" in, the business. In some cases a person might run a business on a part-time basis; he or she might work in the normal way to earn a wage or salary, and run the business outside working hours, perhaps to earn a little extra, or to gain experience. Most people, however, expect to 'earn a living' – their main source of income from their businesses, so their businesses need to be profitable.

If your Business Plan is fair, honest and reasonable, stating the "plain" facts without any adverse factors being hidden, and with no exaggeration, you can gain a good idea of whether or not your proposed business is a "viable" proposition. By this we mean whether or not it stands a good chance of being successful, and profitable. When you are full of enthusiasm for the new business venture, you might be tempted to exaggerate the "plus" factors, and to overlook or ignore "minus" factors, or the "downside". Try to avoid doing that, because an inaccurate Business Plan can be harmful and even worse than not having a plan at all!

Other people whose help you might need (a bank manager or an official of a government agency, for example) will be able to 'study' your Business Plan, and see whether the proposed business has the potential for success. Such people will be experienced in dealing with "new" businesses, and will spot any weaknesses and anything in your Business Plan which does not "ring true". That could count against you, when really their support, guidance and advice could be very valuable to you; so make sure your Business Plan gives a "true picture".

Consequences of NOT preparing a Business Plan.

Never be tempted to neglect the preparation of a Business Plan; it is not a waste of time – it is a valuable guide and business "tool". This practical example will make this very clear to you. In some countries, for a variety of reasons, at one time most businesses were run mainly by just one section of the whole community. However, as circumstances changed, there were better opportunities for one citizen to start, own and run businesses. It is a sad fact that many people started or took over existing businesses without having any business training or experience, and often without sufficient capital (money). Many of these "new" business people faced unexpected difficulties and hardships; many businesses did badly and had to be closed or sold.

Due to a lack of business knowledge and experience too many people started or took over businesses of the same or similar type, often selling similar or even the same products. Very often their businesses were located in the same streets or general areas. This happened in particular with businesses which needed only modest capital and little, if any, knowledge about the products to be sold.

Shops or stores selling ready-to-wear garments are a particular example. In some towns very many such businesses were started and/or taken over, often very close to one another, and often with a number in the same short street all trying to sell virtually identical clothes.

The "new" business people did not realize that an increase in the number of "outlets" (shops or stores) selling the same or similar products does NOT mean that there will automatically be an increase in the numbers of customers who want, need or can afford to buy those products. In fact the opposite is often the case; in a particular area there is usually on a limited number of potential customers for specific types of products.

The numerous clothing shops very soon found themselves in fierce competition with one another, each trying to secure the limited numbers of customers for themselves. To try to do that, they were forced to "cut" (reduce) their prices-often to uneconomic levels to try to "attract customers". In the end, of course, those owners of shops who had limited capital and no reserves, or sources from which to obtain additional capital or which because of the lack of experience or training ran their businesses badly, had to sell (if they could find any buyers) their businesses. Or they had to simply close their businesses down, often losing all their savings.

To make matters worse, other people did not "learn" from the misfortunes. Some of the unprofitable shops were bought or taken over, and the new owners all too often also failed to make them successful. And so they, too, lost both their businesses and their capital.

From this tragic - but true - example we can learn why it is so important for a Business Plan to be prepared to set out - in advance - **the following:-**

❖   The amount of money needed to start the business, how much is available, and whether a "reserve" of money can be "put aside" in case of unforeseen happenings (for example, delays in deliveries, adverse weather).

❖   The "market potential" in a particular area, that is, the number of likely customers in it for the products which it is intended to produce and/or sell.

❖   The existing competition in the area concerned and that competition might have to be faced in the foreseeable future. Competition will reduce the market potential or, at the very least, reduce the profits of a business.

❖   The knowledge, experience, skills and abilities possessed or available to guide the business to success.

In the remainder of this Chapter and in Chapters 2 and 3, we look at each of those important factors in greater detail.

Capital in Starting a Business

One of the most crucial aspects of starting a business is having enough capital to fund your venture. Capital refers to the financial resources that are necessary to start and operate a business. Whether you're starting a small business or a large corporation, having enough capital is essential to cover expenses such as purchasing equipment, hiring employees, leasing office space, and marketing your products or services. In this Section, we will explore the importance of capital for starting a business and discuss various sources of funding that entrepreneurs can consider.

❖   The amount of money needed to start the business, how much is available, and whether a "reserve" of money can be "put aside" in case of unforeseen happenings (for example, delays in deliveries, adverse weather).

❖   The "market potential" in a particular area, that is, the number of likely customers in it for the products which it is intended to produce and/or sell.

❖   The existing competition in the area concerned and that competition might have to be faced in the foreseeable future. Competition will reduce the market potential or, at the very least, reduce the profits of a business.

❖ The knowledge, experience, skills and abilities possessed or available to guide the business to success.

In the remainder of this Chapter and in Chapters 2 and 3, we look at each of those important factors in greater detail.

Capital in Starting a Business

One of the most crucial aspects of starting a business is having enough capital to fund your venture. Capital refers to the financial resources that are necessary to start and operate a business. Whether you're starting a small business or a large corporation, having enough capital is essential to cover expenses such as purchasing equipment, hiring employees, leasing office space, and marketing your products or services. In this Section, we will explore the importance of capital for starting a business and discuss various sources of funding that entrepreneurs can consider.

Capital

When it comes to starting a business, one of the most important factors to consider is capital. Having enough capital to fund your venture is crucial for its success. It is the money you need to invest in equipment, inventory, marketing, and other necessary expenses. Without sufficient capital, it can be challenging to get your business off the ground and sustain it in the long run. In this Chapter, we will discuss the importance of capital for starting a business, different sources of capital, and tips for effectively managing your funds. Read on to learn more about how capital plays a vital role in the success of your business.

The most common reasons why money is needed for new businesses are:

❖ **To pay for machinery and equipment**. Some such items will need to be bought or purchased by most, if not all, new businesses. For example, a bakery will need ovens; a farm will need milking equipment or a tractor; a shop will need desks and chairs, a photocopier, possibly a computer. All such machines, items of equipment and furniture are bought to enable a business to "operate" – to perform its work – smoothly and efficiently. For this reason they are often called "working assets" – the word 'asset' refers to anything which a business owns (including money) – its possessions. Working assets are bought to be "retained" (kept) and used for some years.

❖ **To pay for materials or stocks of goods.** If a business is to make something, it will need materials and/or components from which to make it; for example, the bakery would need flour, yeast and sugar. A trading or distribution business will need to buy goods, which it will then resell to its customers. An office-type business will need paper and envelopes. Once a business has paid for (or agreed to pay for) such items, it legally owns them, so they are also assets; they are often called 'circulating assets', and you will learn why in Chapter Two.)

❖ **To 'meet' or pay its expenses**. Any business will have 'expenses' or 'outgoings' to be paid. The variety of different expenses can be wide, but common ones include rent for the use of premises; telephone, electricity and water charges;

❖ **Postage; advertising; salaries or wages of employees**. As we have already mentioned, often some of these expenses have to be paid even before a business starts operating and "earning" income.

Practical Example A:

Let us put all these factors together, and consider a "practical" situation. Martha Albert has worked for other people for years as a dressmaker/seamstress, earning a wage. She has become an expert needlewoman. She has noticed that more and more people buy "off the peg" garments from clothing shops/stores, rather than having clothes specially "made to measure" (which is much more expensive.)

However, clothes are manufactured in only the most popular and rather limited "sizes" (waist, leg lengths, chest/bust sizes, sleeve lengths, and so on.) She has noticed that many people buy "ready to wear" clothes, but find that the garments do not always fit exactly; perhaps the waist is too tight or too loose, or the legs are too long or too short. People need their garments to be altered to fit them better.

So Martha has an "idea". She decides to start a business offering a service to alter clothes (to fit their owners better) and also to repair damage to clothes, such as rips or tears or broken zips.

Martha cannot work from her home, so she must find suitable 'premises' (or "accommodation") in a building from which to run her business. She will have to pay rent to the owner of the premises for the right to use them. She will need to buy a sewing machine (maybe more than one) and a 'pressing' or ironing machine. She will have to "furnish" the premises; she might need to decorate them; to paint the walls and ceiling, to lay suitable flooring, to build a "changing room", to install mirrors, and so on. She will need at least one table and chair, and perhaps a counter at which to attend to customers. She will need an electricity supply to operate her machines and for lighting (perhaps also heating or cooling). She will need water, she will need a telephone.

She will need to buy many different materials, such as different colors of cotton thread, buttons, pins and needles, and zips. She will need to buy "tools", such as pairs of scissors and measuring tapes. Martha will only gain customers if **(1)** they know about the services her business offers, and **(2)** they know how to find where the business is "located" – where it is. She can give that information by "word of mouth" to some people, such as friends and relatives. But she needs to "reach" more people, and she does that by paying to advertise, perhaps in her local newspaper or on social media or local radio, on in leaflets (flyers) or posters printed and distributed to possible customers. She will need a sign with the name of the business somewhere on the outside of the building, so customers can find her premises).

You can see that Martha needs to spend a lot of money, even before her business "opens its doors" and starts providing services to its customers, for which they will pay. And at this stage she does not know for certain that she will gain customers, or sufficient customers to pay "back" all the money she has already spent and needs to spend in the future; for example, she will have to pay the agreed amount of rent every single month, without fail.

Then, too, if she feels she will not be able herself to do all the work necessary to "satisfy" her customers, and also run the business, she might have to employ – and pay wages or salaries to one or more other people. An additional salary or wage is not only a heavy expenses for the business, but also involves considerable additional "paperwork" in making and accounting for deductions for income tax, social security/national insurance contributions, etc.

Sources of Capital

Starting a business requires more than just a great idea and a passion for success. One of the biggest challenges entrepreneurs face is finding the necessary capital to get their business off the ground. Luckily, there are several sources of capital available for aspiring business owners. Whether it's through traditional lenders, venture capitalists, crowdfunding platforms, or personal savings, understanding the different options for funding is essential for any entrepreneur. In this blog post, we will explore the various sources of capital and discuss their advantages and disadvantages, helping you make informed decisions as you embark on your entrepreneurial journey.

Savings

People, who have been in employment, earning a wage or salary, might sometimes have earned more than they needed to spend at once. They might have been able to "put aside" or to save some of their earnings. Their 'savings', as they are called, might be "deposited" for safekeeping in a bank or a building society, or a similar "financial institution", As more money is deposited from time to time, the total value of the savings "grows".

Some people "inherit" money from deceased parents or other relatives. Some might receive "redundancy pay" if their jobs are lost. Some might receive "pensions" from previous employment. All such people might deposit amounts of money which are in "excess" of their immediate needs with banks, etc.

Banks and building societies usually pay a bonus, which is called 'interest', to customers who deposit money with them. The amount of the interest which is "earned" is added to the amount of savings, thus increasing it. Of course, savings might be used for other things, but often a person is able to save enough money over a period of time to use as the capital for his or her business, or at least as part of the total amount of capital needed.

No doubt you have already tried to 'save' towards the cost of your business, but if not, it might not be too late to start!

Loans

Money which is borrowed from other people or businesses with the intention that it will be "paid back" or "repaid" at a later date, is called a **'loan'.** The money is said to be "lent" or "loaned. The person or business who lends the money is called the **'lender'.** The person or business to whom or to which the money is loaned is called the **'borrower'.**

Sometimes a person wishing to start a business might be able to obtain a loan from a relative or from a friend, or perhaps a number of loans from different relatives and friends. If you are in this situation, it is important that money is not accepted unless you have the definite intention to repay it in due course. Bad feelings can result if money borrowed is not repaid as and when promised.

Alternatively, a bank (or building society) might be approached for a loan. If you have already been a customer of the bank, and better still a "saver" with that bank, your approach might be looked on more favorably by the manager of the "local" branch of the bank. A bank is a business and, like any other business, its main objective is to make profits for its owners. It cannot risk losing money by loaning or lending money to just anybody for just any reason. It is to loan money for a business venture, a sound "business proposition" must be made.

First of all the bank manager (or a subordinate) will want to have details of your proposed business; in fact a copy of the Business Plan (which we have already considered.) If you can offer for inspection a fair and honest, well considered Business Plan, then you will get off on the "right footing". The bank official will no doubt want to study and discuss the Plan with you, and might be able to give you sound "financial advice", based on his or her experience with many other business "startups".

Obviously the bank official will need to know how much – the 'sum'- you want to know, and for how long. It might surprise you to know that a bank manager might even want to be sure that the sum you are asking to borrow is not too low! That is because some "new" business people are too modest in their calculations. They might not take "into account" all the many and varied types of expenses which will have to be met. They might not have made provision for times when business is "slack", or when it is interrupted by unforeseen events; by a strike by transport workers, or severe weather conditions, to give you just too examples. These are times when a 'reserve' is needed. So it might be wise to ask to borrow slightly more, rather than less.

The bank will set out in a document the "conditions" under which a loan might be offered. In addition to the sum of money which might be loaned, the document will cover other matters of great importance to the borrower.

Term of the Loan

The bank might agree to lend the sum of money over a period of one year, or two or three years, or longer. The period is called the 'term'. A "short-term" (say one year or two years) loan might seem attractive, but a new business person must be confident the new business will earn enough soon enough, because the loan will have to be repaid during that short period.

Repayment

Perhaps a certain amount of the sum borrowed might have to be repaid every month or every "quarter" (three months) or every half-year (six months) or every year. For example, say the sum of $30,000 is loaned to you by a bank; you- the borrower – might have to repay the sum of $2,500 each month for 12 months, or $1,250 each month for 24 months. Sometimes, the whole sum borrowed might have to be repaid at one time after a stated period. You MUST allow for the repayment of any loan in your calculations and Business Plan.

Security or Collateral

To reduce the risk of losing money, a bank will usually require the borrower to make a "pledge" that in the event of all or part of the sum loaned not being repaid as agreed, the bank may seize instead some property (possession) of the borrower; that is called 'security' or 'collateral'. Rarely will a bank loan be made without suitable security or collateral.

The security or collateral for a loan which can be offered will, of course, depend on the individual, and how much – how large in value – is the sum of the loan asked for. It might be a person's house, or a piece of land owned, or a motor vehicle, and so on. If you are a new business person starting a business with a bank loan, you must realize that there is a risk, should the business not succeed.

Instead of asking for security, or in addition to security, the bank might require another person of standing to 'guarantee' the loan. This means that in the event of the business not succeeding that person – the 'guarantor' – can also be pursued by the bank to pay all or part of the loan not repaid by the borrower.

Interest

A bank (like any other business) charges it customers for the services it provides to them. If it agrees to lend money, then it will charge for doing so – that charge is called 'interest'. The bank charges a certain 'rate' of interest, which is usually presented as a percentage, such as 5 per cent or 8 per cent of the sum loaned. The term 'per cent' means 'of a hundred', and is often shown by the % sign; for example 5% or 8%. These mean "five one-hundredths" and "eight one-hundredths". The rate of interest is sometimes stated as being "per annum" – which might be abbreviated to "pa"- meaning "for each year". So, for instance, if you were to borrow the sum of $15,000 from a bank at the rate of 5% "per annum" (per year) interest of $750-5 one-hundredths of $15,000 – would have to be paid to the bank each year. At 8%, the sum of $1,200 in interest would have to be paid to the bank each year.

If the sum borrowed is large, then the amount of interest payable can be high. The interest payable will be an expense of the business, and so will reduce profits made. Interest might be payable monthly or quarterly or "annually" ("yearly"). For example, if the annual amount of interest is $570, you might have to pay US$62.50 "per" (each) month, or US$187.50 per quarter. Sometimes, the rate of interest is "fixed" during the term of the loan; sometimes it is "variable", which means that it might rise, or might fall. If the rate falls, less interest is payable; if it rises, higher interest is payable.

In some countries different banks, building societies and other "financial institutions" may offer loans (as well as overdraft facilities – see next section) at different – competitive – rates of interest, so it might be worth "shopping around" to find the best "deal".

Do NOT forget that the interest has to be paid in addition to the agreed repayments of the loan.

Loan Agreement

If you want to borrow money you must consider carefully the "conditions" on which the bank will lend to you. It might be possible for you to obtain advice from an accountant or a business advisor before agreeing to accept the bank's offer. Sometimes there might even be the chance to "negotiate" – to "bargain", as it were to get better conditions, for instance a lower interest rate, or a longer period of loan. Also, if there are competing banks in your country (and that is not always the case in all countries) it might be wise to approach more than one bank, and to compare what each offers.

The final conditions – set out in a document under which a loan is offered by a bank have to be signed by both a representative of the bank and by the borrower (and the signatures usually have to be "witnessed" by other people.) Once the document has been properly signed by both "parties" (bank and borrower) it becomes a legally 'binding agreement'. If either party fails to carry out the agreed obligations, for example, if the borrower fails to pay interest or to repay the loan, the other party can take legal action to recover the money. *So do think carefully before you resort to a bank loan.*

Bank Overdraft

This is another facility which a bank might offer, but usually only to an existing customer who has had a good "record" in operating his or her account with that bank. It is NOT a "loan", as we have described above. What it means is that the bank allows the customer to 'withdraw' (take out) more money from the bank than that customer has deposited with the bank, that is, to 'over draw'. For example, say you have a "balance" of $1,200 in your account with a bank. The bank might, perhaps, permit you to withdraw (usually by means of documents called **cheques or checks,** which we discuss in Chapter Two) up to a maximum of $5,000 in addition to the $1,200 at any one time. So you could issue a **cheques or checks** or a number of **cheques or checks** for a total of up to $6,200.

The bank charges interest on the amount 'overdrawn', usually on a daily basis, although the interest might only be charged to the account every month or quarter. For instance, the first cheque you issue might be for only $1,400, so the amount overdrawn (on which interest will be charged) is only $200. The next cheque or checks issued might be for $920, and so the amount overdrawn (on which interest will be charged) will increase to $1,120. And so on. An advantage of an overdraft is that as and when money is deposited with (or paid into) the bank, the amount of the overdraft (on which interest will be charged) decreases.

But there are also significant disadvantages, which you must consider:-

❖   The rate of interest charged on an overdraft is often higher than for a loan. As and when interest is charged (or "credited") to the "overdrawn" account, it increases the total amount overdrawn – on which further interest will be charged.

❖   Whereas a loan is for an agreed "term", an overdraft is NOT. The bank can insist on the repayment of or "call in" the amount overdrawn at any time, without warning. That could be very serious for you and your business if you had no alternative (other) source of funds from which to repay the bank.

The agreement of the bank must be obtained before a bank account is overdrawn. The bank will state the conditions (which will have to be accepted and signed) under which the overdraft may be "operated". They will cover the maximum amount which may ever be overdrawn and the rate of interest (which will vary or "fluctuate".) The bank might also, especially if the overdraft might be large, insist on having security or collateral, and/or a guarantor.

You might find a short-term overdraft facility beneficial if interest rates are low, and if you have a regular source of income (e.g. salary or a pension) to help keep down the amount overdrawn. But it is not usually wise to rely on an overdraft in the long-term. And remember: an overdraft is NOT a loan.

Business Development Organizations

Business development organizations (BDOs) play a crucial role in supporting and fostering the growth of businesses, particularly small and medium-sized enterprises (SMEs). BDOs are non-profit entities that aim to stimulate economic development by providing resources, guidance, and networking opportunities to businesses. They serve as a bridge between entrepreneurs, government agencies, and other stakeholders, facilitating the creation of partnerships and collaborations that drive innovation and create jobs. In this chapter, we will explore the role and significance of BDOs in supporting business growth and economic prosperity.

Many of these business development organizations including those which are semi-government or quasi-government run are able to provide forms of "financial assistance" to aspiring business people. Some might be able to provide 'interest-free loans' or 'low-interest loans' or 'grants' towards all or part of the capital needed to establish a new business, or for the purchase of specific assets. Of course, a sound Business Plan is usually required before any form of assistance will be considered.

Even if "direct" financial assistance is not available for your business venture, the backing of such an organization will usually lend support to an approach you might make to a bank for a loan. Or you might be advised about which other organization(s) might be able to assist you financially.

Contribution to Capital other than Money

Sometimes, instead of actual money – "cash" – alone, an intending business person might have something which is worth money, or which has what is called *'monetary value' or 'monetary worth'*. For example, a person might own a plot of land on which vegetables for sale can be grown. Another person might have a structure in his or her house or nearby, which can be used as a workshop, or as a store for products, or as an office. In other cases people might own equipment or tools which can be used by the new business. Such facilities are "worth money", because they save actual money having to be spent (for example, on renting premises, or on buying equipment or tools, and so on.) So the amount of actual money needed to start a particular business might be lower than otherwise. If you own an asset or assets (in addition to money) which could be useful to a new business, this might be a matter worth considering (if you have not already done that.) And especially if you have not yet decided what type of business to start, or from where to operate your business.

Combinations of Sources of Capital

In practice, many people find it necessary to raise the initial capital and/or the total capital they need from a combination of different sources. For example, you might have some savings "put aside", and/or you might be able to secure a grant from a business development agency, but even then might need to "top up" with a loan from a bank or elsewhere.

Limiting Costs

Once you have decided – based on the funds forecast in your Business Plan- the amount of initial capital you will need to start (or buy) your business, you should next consider the sources of "funds" which are or might be available to you. Then, depending on how much you will need to get the business started and operational (plus a "reserve", as explained) you should undertake research to compare costs; for example, interest charged on a bank loan is often lower than on an overdraft and, furthermore, some banks or other financial organizations might charge lower rates of interest than others charge. Having done your "research", try to raise the amount of capital you need at the least practicable costs, in order to limit the "drain" on your resources which payments of interest and loan repayments will cause.

CHAPTER QUESTIONS ONE – CHAPTER 1

Recommended Answers to the Questions-against which you may compare your answers-are in the Appendix after the end of this Chapter. The maximum mark which may be awarded for each Question appears in brackets at the end of the Question.

No.1. What is a "business plan", and why is it so important that you should prepare one before starting a business? (maximum 40 marks)

No.2. (a) What is the "capital" of a business? Describe the main types of expenses which might have to be paid before a business is started. (maximum 20 marks)

(b) With regard to a bank loan, explain what you understand by the "term", the "rate of interest", and "security" or "collateral". (maximum 20 marks)

No.3. Place a tick in the box **v** against the one correct statement in each set.
(a) In business, the term "goods" refers to:
1.☐ payment which is received in exchange for efficient work performed.
2.☐ the highest quality of items which a business hopes to sell.
3.☐ physical items which a business offers for sale to customers.
4.☐ money spent wisely on expenses such as rent, salaries and services.

(b) It is safest to start the type of business which:
1.☐ does not need any skill or previous experience.
2.☐ depends on the skill of people other than its owner(s).
3.☐ needs much capital because it will be more valuable.
4.☐ you have the skills and experience to run successfully.

(c) A bank overdraft:

1.☐ allows a bank's customer to draw out more money than that customer has deposited with the bank.

2.☐ is simply another name for a bank loan.

3.☐ is cheaper in interest than a bank loan.

4.☐ has to be repaid in regular sums over a period of time, called its "term".

(d) The main types of business activities:

1.☐ are selling, buying and distributing.

2.☐ are manufacturing, trading/distribution and service-providing.

3.☐ are small, medium, large and very large.

4.☐ goods and services.

(e)Assets are:

1.☐ the capital of a business.

2.☐ what a business owns; its possessions.

3.☐ animals reared by farmers to be used as beasts of burden.

4.☐ what a business pays out; its expenses.

No.4. Place a tick in the box **v** against the one correct statement in each set.

(a) A profit is made by a business when:

1.☐ the total of its income is greater than the total of its expenditure.

2.☐ its owner has raised all the capital needed to start it.

3.☐ the total of its expenditure is greater than the total of its income.

4.☐ a bank agrees to make a low-interest loan to it.

(b) Plans are necessary in business:

1.☐ so its owner can find his or her way to work each day.

2.☐ to transport goods to its customers all over the country.

3.☐ to pay for machinery and equipment it needs to operate smoothly.

4.☐ to guide it to the achievement of its objectives.

(c) Competition for a business:

1.☐ increases the numbers of customers for the products it sells.
2.☐ decreases the number of customers for the products it sells.
3.☐ increases the price which it must charge for the products it sells.
4.☐ makes no difference to the number of customers for its products.

(d) Bank interest

1.☐ means that a customer has money deposited with a bank.
2.☐ means that the bank is keen to help a business succeed.
3.☐ is received on money deposited, but paid on money borrowed.
4.☐ means that a bank is anxious to secure you as a customer.

(e) The initial capital of a business:

1.☐ is the pieces or location from which its operations are first
   conducted.
2.☐ is always raised from a bank loan and/or a bank draft.
3.☐ is required to meet expenses which have to be incurred before it
   starts earning sufficient income from its activities.
4.☐ is not required until after it has commenced operations.

(2 marks for a statement correctly ticked – maximum 20 marks

Chapter 2
BUSINESS OWNERSHIP

Introduction

A business is an entity. Ownership of a business refers to the legal rights and responsibilities of an individual or group of individuals who have control over the assets and operations of the company. Understanding the concept of ownership is essential for anyone interested in starting or managing a business. This chapter provides an introduction to the different types of business ownership, including sole proprietorship, partnership, and corporation, as well as the advantages and disadvantages of each. Whether you are a budding entrepreneur or a seasoned business professional, gaining a clear understanding of ownership is crucial for making informed decisions and ensuring the success of your business.

A business exists, but much of it is intangible. We might be able to see and touch some of its assets, such as currency notes and coins, machines, or stocks of goods for sale. We might be able to see the premises (the building from which it operates. We might be able to see the person or people who run it. But there is much that we cannot see or touch: the skills, knowledge, experience or client; the activities which go on "behind the scenes". Ownership of a business can consist of more than one person. The business is likely to consist of both tangible and intangible parts. Just one person might own the "whole", or the ownership – not the business itself – might be shared between two or more people.

Defining business ownership: What it means to own a business

To truly grasp the concept of business ownership, it is important to consider what it means to own a business. Owning a business entails more than just having legal rights and responsibilities over its assets and operations. It encompasses the ability to make important decisions, take risks, and derive financial benefits from the enterprise's success. Ownership grants individuals or groups control and authority over the direction of the business. This includes the power to determine the company's strategies, set goals, hire and manage employees, and allocate resources effectively. It also involves shouldering the liability and risks associated with the business.

However, business ownership is not only about personal gains. It also requires a commitment to the well-being of all stakeholders, such as employees, customers, and the community. Owners must prioritize ethical practices and ensure the long-term sustainability and growth of the business.

In our next section, we will discuss the various types of business ownership in greater detail, examining their unique characteristics and implications. Stay tuned to gain further insight into this crucial aspect of entrepreneurship.

Legal and financial responsibilities of business owners

Business owners have several legal and financial responsibilities that they must fulfill to operate their businesses effectively. Legally, business owners must comply with various requirements, including obtaining the necessary permits and licenses, filing taxes correctly and timely, and complying with labor and employment laws.

Financially, business owners must manage their financial obligations, including paying taxes, managing debts, keeping accurate financial records, and ensuring that their business's financial health is sustainable. Failure to fulfill these responsibilities can result in legal action, including fines, lawsuits, and even bankruptcy. Business owners must understand and fulfill their legal and financial obligations to ensure the smooth operation of their businesses and avoid legal problems.

The benefits and challenges of business ownership

Business ownership has both benefits and challenges. On the one hand, owning a small business allows individuals a degree of independence and freedom to make their own decisions. Business owners also have the opportunity to turn skills, interests and passions into income, while also contributing to the economy through job creation. On the other hand, challenges such as financial instability, high levels of responsibility and stress can make business ownership difficult and require significant personal sacrifices. Furthermore, business owners may face difficulties such as struggling to balance work with their personal life and finding the right people to help them grow their business.

How to establish ownership of a business
To establish ownership of a business, there are several steps you can take;

Determine Your Business Concept: Clearly define the type of business you want to start and the products or services you will offer.

Research Your Competitors and Market: Conduct market research to understand your target audience, competitive landscape, and industry trends.

Create Your Business Plan: Develop a comprehensive business plan that outlines your goals, strategies, financial projections, and marketing plans.

Choose Your Business Structure: Decide on the legal structure of your business, such as sole proprietorship, partnership, or corporation. Each structure has different implications for ownership and liability.

Register Your Business and Get Licenses: Register your business with the appropriate government authorities and obtain any necessary licenses and permits to operate legally.

Get a Tax Identification Number: Apply for a tax identification number, such as an Employer Identification Number (EIN), which will be used for tax purposes and to open a business bank account.

Establish Bank Accounts: Open a separate bank account for your business to keep personal and business finances separate.

Secure Funding: Determine how you will finance your business, whether through personal savings, loans, or investments from others.

Obtain Business Insurance: Protect your business and its assets by obtaining the necessary insurance coverage, such as general liability insurance or professional liability insurance.

Develop Contracts and Agreements: Create contracts and agreements that outline the ownership rights, responsibilities, and expectations of all parties involved, such as partnership agreements or shareholder agreements.

Maintain Proper Recordkeeping: Keep accurate financial records and ensure compliance with tax and legal requirements. Implement a system for tracking income, expenses, and other financial transactions.

By following these steps, you can establish ownership of your business and lay the foundation for its success.

Tips for successful business ownership
Here are some guides for successful business ownership:

Develop a solid business plan: A well-thought-out business plan helps you define your goals, target market, and strategies for growth. It also serves as a roadmap for your business.

Understand your target market: Identify your target customers, understand their needs, and tailor your products or services to meet those needs. Conduct market research to gather insights and stay updated on market trends.

Build a strong team: Surround yourself with talented individuals who share your vision and can contribute to the success of your business. Delegate tasks, empower your team, and foster a positive work culture.

Prioritize customer satisfaction: Focus on providing exceptional customer service and building long-lasting relationships with your customers. Listen to their feedback and continuously improve your products or services to meet their expectations.

Stay adaptable and innovative: Embrace change and be open to new ideas. Be willing to adjust your strategies and products/services based on market demands. Stay updated on industry trends and technology advancements to stay ahead of the competition.

Manage your finances wisely: Keep track of your expenses and revenue, and maintain a sound financial management system. Monitor cash flow, budget effectively, and seek professional advice when needed.

Stay committed and persevere: Running a business is not easy, and there will be challenges and setbacks along the way. Stay focused, stay motivated, and be willing to put in the hard work required to achieve your goals.

Network and build relationships: Establish connections within your industry, attend industry events, and join business organizations. Networking can help you learn from others, gain new business opportunities, and expand your customer base.

Embrace technology: Utilize technology tools and platforms to streamline your operations, improve efficiency, and reach a wider audience. Embrace digital marketing strategies to promote your business and engage with customers online.

Continuously learn and adapt: Stay updated on industry news, emerging trends, and new business strategies. Invest in your own personal and professional development to stay ahead in the competitive business world.

Remember, successful business ownership requires passion, hard work, and continuous learning. Trust your instincts, take calculated risks, and never stop striving for improvement.

The role and significance of business ownership in the economy
Business ownership plays a crucial role in the economy as it fuels economic growth and development. Entrepreneurs who own businesses are responsible for creating job opportunities, stimulating innovation, and driving competition in markets. Through their businesses, owners inject capital into the economy, which helps fund new projects and stimulates the growth of existing businesses. They also create wealth and generate tax revenue for governments, which helps to fund public services and infrastructure.

Additionally, business ownership drives innovation and creativity, as entrepreneurs seek to develop new products, services, and technologies to meet changing consumer needs. This, in turn, helps boost consumer spending and drives economic growth.

Overall, business ownership is a key driver of economic development, creating employment opportunities, generating capital, and stimulating innovation and development.

The Profit Motivation

People start, own and run businesses with one common "goal" in mind. And that is to make money from the activities of their respective businesses. Many business people are content to earn a reasonable "living" so that they and their family will have a good "standard of living". Other business people want to earn "big money", to be successful and respected' perhaps to retire young. They are all motivated by the need to make profits from their businesses.

Of course, there may be other "motivation": the challenge to do something new or different, perhaps what has not been done before; the chance to exercise skill or judgement' the stimulation of taking "risks", to out-think others; to work for oneself, to mention but a few.

The motivations which prompt people to go into business are often summed up as being the "entrepreneurial spirit". What we call an 'entrepreneur' (adapted from a French word) is commonly defined as being:

A person who undertakes a commercial or business venture, with the chance of making a profit or a loss, and often at personal or financial RISK.

For success in business, an entrepreneur needs to be self-confident and resourceful; to be able to focus, concentrate and persevere; to be able to
analyze (to understand and see through the maze of distractions); and he or she also needs flexibility of mind, good judgement and the ability to take – the right – decisions; and, of course, commitment.

The common aim of most entrepreneurs is profit. So let us be quite clear how and why profits arise. The following simple example explains clearly to you what profit is really is and how it arises. It is important for you to understand these matters clearly if you are to make a successful career in business.

Practical Example: B

Rebecca Fraser is a fashion designer; he runs a small business called "Rebecca Collection" from a workshop he rents. She sells ladies handbags she has made, and the money she receives goes towards buying food or clothing or buying materials or paying the rent of her workshop. What she has done is to exchange her materials and labour for the materials and labour of other people; what we call "money" (currency or bank notes and coins) is only the "medium" which makes the exchange easier.

In order to design and produce ladies handbags, Rebecca has to make use of what are called the "three factors of production'; they are: land, labour and capital. ***That is because:-***

❖   *without land there would be no place or workshop in which she could work;*
❖   *without her labour no ladies handbags would be made;* without capital there would not be the money which she need to pay rent of her workshop, to buy leather, tools, nails, etc, from which she can design and produce more ladies handbags, and to feed and clothe herself and any dependents until the next ladies handbags are designed and made and sold.

Rebecca works hard in the expectation that her production will bring back the money she spends on materials, on labour, and on rent, and that it will also bring her more than the total she spent. The "return" on the capital she "invests" is what is called "profit". A 'return on capital' in the form of profit is essential in business. That is because capital is really the result of previous production. If Rebecca works so well that she sells her products for more money than her immediate needs, she can use that extra or excess money as capital to 'finance' more production. We can explain that a business 'makes a profit' from its activities or operations during a certain period, **when:**

❖   the total of all its **'income'** – its receipts of money –
exceeds (is greater than)
❖   the total of all its **'expenditure'** – its payments out of money.

The amount of the excess of income over expenditure represents a profit made by the business. The "period" we mentioned is called a 'trading period' or a 'financial period', and is most often a one year period: a "trading year" or "financial year". That is not necessarily the same as a "calendar year", e.g. from January 1 to December 31. Commonly the trading or financial year of a business is counted as 12 months from the first day of the month on which it was established. For instance, if a business was started on July 1, each of its financial or trading years might be from July 1 in one year to June 30 in the following year.

Losses in Business

In business a 'loss' is the opposite of a profit. Say the total expenditure of a business exceeds (is greater than) the total of its income during a certain financial or trading period. The amount of the excess of expenditure over income represents a loss made by – or incurred by – the business. We say that the business has 'lost money' during its activities and operations.

If a business continues to make losses, its capital will be used up, and if the owner cannot raise more capital, the business will become 'insolvent' and will have to close. It goes without saying that every business person strives to avoid making losses! And this Program aims to help you avoid such a unfortunate situation occurring.

Different Types of Business Ownership Structures

Understanding the different types of business ownership structures is essential for aspiring entrepreneurs and existing business owners alike. People who are business take certain risks. For example, if a business does not do well, its owner(s) might lose the money and effort they invested in it. People who own and run businesses also have certain obligations; there are things which they must do, and there are things which they must not do, morally or legally

In this Chapter you will learn how to reduce business risks and ways to avoid losses; and how to ensure that moral and legal business obligations are met. The way in which a particular business is owned can have important effects on the risks and obligations of its owner(s).

We can now look at each business ownership structure; as it each business ownership structure comes with its own set of characteristics, legal requirements, and implications. By exploring these options, you can choose the ownership structure that best aligns with your goals, values, and resources.

The most common types of business ownership structures include sole proprietorships, partnerships, limited liability companies (LLCs), and corporations. It is possible to change, or convert from one type of ownership to another, even after a business has been registered. Let's take a closer look at each:

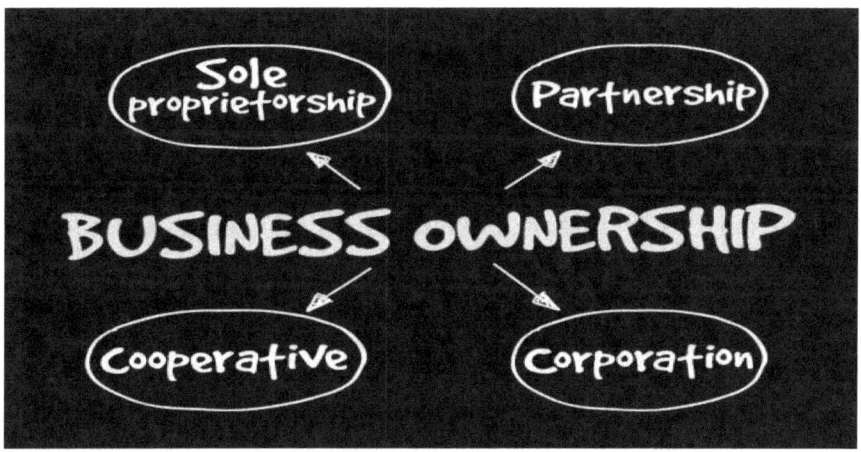

Sole proprietorship:

This is the simplest form of business ownership, where an individual owns and operates the business as a sole owner. The word "sole" means alone or one person only. It shows that a business of this type is owned by just one person. You might hear the expressions sole-trader or sole-proprietor or one man business or self-employed. The sole-owner might be either a man or a woman.

The sole-proprietorship business is usually fairly small with wide range of and the range of activities:-

❖ *many are in engaged in trading and distribution.*
❖ *some are engaged in small-scale manufacturing or in agriculture.*
❖ *many are engaged in technical or crafts fields, as motor mechanics, electricians, radio or television engineers, painters and decorators, fashion designers, etc; some provide domestic services, such as gardening, window or carpet cleaning, etc.*

❖ *some provide commercial services, like estate agents, insurance agents, couriers and road transporters, taxis or cabs or minibuses, etc.*

❖ *some are concerned with running cafés, restaurants, guest houses and small hotels.*

The management of sole proprietorship is generally fairly simple as the owner or manager will know personally each person working in the business. The owner will normally have a good knowledge of the work performed by each person. In some small businesses certain specialists with important skills, knowledge or experience might have to be employed.

Advantages of Sole proprietorship

- *The owner retains all profits made by the business.*
- *The owner makes all decisions, and does not have to consult anybody else.*
- *The owner has ease of control of the business and personal contact with customers and suppliers.*

Disadvantages of Sole proprietorship
There are also disadvantages to being a sole proprietor, which include:-

- The owner might find it difficult to take holidays, without having to close the business.

- If the owner falls ill or has suffered an injury, the business will not operate and will have to close until the owner is capable of resuming work.

- A sole proprietor might not have all the knowledge and skill required to run a business successfully, and might not have the time to carry out all the managerial functions necessary.

- A sole proprietor might have problem in generating the initial capital needed to start the business properly, and also in raising funds needed to keep the business going in difficult times or expands it.

- The owner also assumes unlimited personal liability and is personally responsible for the business's debts. What this means is if the owner has insufficient money, his or her personal possessions such as house, car, furniture, etc. could be confiscated through legal means and sold to offset the debts of the business.

Registration of Business Name

This type of business unit is relatively easy to set up. A government body is responsible for registration of the intended business name in many countries. In some countries, the "Registrar of Business Names", under the Ministry of Trade or Commerce or Industry (or similar) is responsible for registration of business names.

For example, if John wants to register a business name. He might like to call the intended business "Daily Associate Agency". John might have to approach a local government office or local chamber of commerce for advice. He may be required to complete a simple application form and submit, perhaps with a small registration fee, to the Registrar of Business Names. Apart from the name of the business John wants to register, he will also, have to state his own name and address as the owner-to-be, in addition to the type of activities in which the business will be engaged, and additional information, such as the intended business address from which the business will operate.

If the name of the intended business, John has chosen is very similar to another business already registered he will not be permitted to register his first choice. He will have to select a different name and might be issued a 'registration certificate' after the chosen name has been approved. Once he has the registration certificate, he might have to display the registration certificate prominently in his business premises, as proof his business is legally registered to operate.

Converting a Sole-Proprietorship Business into a Partnership Business

Some businesses start as sole-proprietorship and expand into partnership. To develop into partnership firms from a sole proprietorship, the initial process is to draft the partnership business deed. The deed will include conditions of the business, the partnership start-up date and relationship between the partners.

It must be indicated in the deed how much capital will each partner invest, how the profits and losses will be split and what happens after retirement to one or more partners. In the deed there should be details of all the changes expected to occur with the introduction of the new business partners. It includes any change in the firm's registered address details as well.

When you convert a sole proprietorship to a partnership, there will be a change in the structure. Each partner has effective and equal control over the activities of the business and shares profits equally unless there is any agreement contrary to this in the partnership agreement. A partner must not transfer their interest to others without other existing partners' consensus.

The partnership business will make declaration of transfer deed which is different from a regular partnership deed. The declaration of transfer deed will make several references to the proprietorship business and will declare the transfer to a partnership firm. The declaration of transfer deeds must include the date of sole proprietorship formation, name of sole proprietor, type of business, TIN, Tax registration and VAT numbers.

The partners can jointly agree to choose any name for their partnership firm and register it with the Registrar of Business Names. There is no government mandatory set of rules for naming the firm. The partners should make sure that the name given is not already registered by another business.

There should be mutual agreement between partners which, each partner will be bound by the actions of the other partners. Hence, with a mutual agreement, the partners act as the principals of the other partners.

Note that whenever a partner leaves the partnership firm, a new business is formed. Any time a new partner is admitted to a partnership, a new business is formed and new partnership agreements are required. The Registrar of business must be informed about changes in ownership of a partnership firm.

Partnership Firms

In a partnership, two or more individuals share ownership and control of the business. Partners contribute resources, share profits and losses, and collectively make decisions. Depending on the type of partnership, partners may have limited liability or be personally liable for the business's obligations.

This type of business unit is usually governed by a legal agreement in writing called a' partnership agreement' which outline the duties and responsibilities of each partner. The partnership agreement will also outlines what proportion or percentage of the business each of the owners "owns" what earnings each may receive, and how any profits or gains made by the business will be shared between the partners. In some cases people go into partnership with spoken agreement between them which is very dangerous form of partnership. This type of partnership can lead to misunderstanding, disputes, losses and unpleasantness.

Some people might trust each other such; as close relatives, brothers or sisters. It is important for them to sign a legally binding partnership agreement. An attorney of law or an accountant should be able to assist and advise in this regards. There are standard worded prepared agreements which set out the most common matters which need to be included; such as the names and addresses of the partners, the name of their firm, and the methods in which they are to share ownership, earnings and profits or losses. All of the above details need to be filled in the agreement before it is signed and witnessed.

Apart from attorney of law and accountants mentioned above. There are other professionals such as auditors, doctors, dentists, architects, civil engineers and others, who do not consider their profession as business, but they rarely provide services without charge, and sometimes, similar professionals work together as partners with the common goal of earning money and, making profits and might call their unit a practice instead of a firm.

Reasons for Forming a Partnership

In some cases two or more persons might join together to form or take over or a run a business by pooling their skills, knowledge, experience, contacts, finance, assets; or combination of any of the above factors. This type of business unit is commonly run by husband and wife as a team, and the business can be any of the followings: cafés, restaurants, guesthouses and small hotels, hairdressing salons, travel agencies and estate agencies. The partners might not have the time or fund to run a successful partnership business. But they can do the followings:-

❖ *share the work, and pool their expertise or resources together; and*
❖ *might be able to earn a modest income and enjoy good standard of living or a useful second income.*

In some cases, whereby persons forming partnership business might not have sufficient knowledge, skill or finance to run a business; two or more persons can pool their knowledge, talents and resources and work together as a partnership team, and might be able to run a successful business. In many cases, one or more of the partners might provide the skill, experience or technical know-how, whilst one or more others might some or all of the capital needed.

Sources of Capital

In a partnership firm, some partners are involved in day to day running of the business, whilst some might provide all or part of the fund needed and leave the day to day running of the business to the working partners. Partners who do not partake in day to day running of the partnership business are called *sleeping partners.*

In some cases, some partnership firm has 50/50 partnership or an equal partnership. But, some partners might not necessarily contribute the same amount of capital. For instance, one partner might raise two-thirds of the capital needed, whilst another might raise the remaining one third. In fact, there is no fixed rule, and much depends on the circumstances, and what is agreed between the partners.

Division of Profits

Depending on the proportions agreed in the partnership agreement. Any profits made by a partnership firm are divided between all the partners in that firm. The division might be based on amounts or percentages of capital contributed or on work performed, on time devoted to the business.

Liability for Losses

If the partnership firm has been incorporated, the liability of each partner for the debts of the firm is limited. Any losses made by a partnership firm are shared between all the partners in that firm. In some cases, a wealthy partner of a partnership firm could take personal responsibility in settling any of the debts of the business, which the other partners are unable to meet.

Advantages of Partnerships
Advantages of partnership firms might include:-

❖   One of the biggest challenges of starting a new partnership business is the overhead expenses. Partners can share startup costs and other expenses.

❖   There is the possibility to spread the workload and responsibilities of the business among the partners, and at the same time allowing different
partners to focus on their areas of specialization, thereby, providing access to essential skills and experience within the business.

❖   One partner can cover for another partner in absence of one partner due to holiday or illness. If one partner is no longer interested in the partnership and want to leave the partnership, the partners can apply partnership interests' agreement to transfer the right to receive benefits to a new partner. With a partnership, there will be less pressure in handling day to day detail of the business. In this instance, having a partner can improve both partner's work–life and routine.

❖ In a business partnership, a partner with a different perspective can provide valuable input when making important decisions.

❖ It easy to change a partnership business into other business structures, if the partners decide that they need more protection for their business. To start the conversion process from partnership to a limited liability company or corporation, they must submit official conversion documents to the Registrar of Business Office.

❖ Business partnership enjoys more freedom when it comes to ownership and control in equal measure than limited liability company or corporation. Members of business partnership are only answerable only to each other and without outside influence in decision making.

Disadvantages of Partnerships

❖ In some cases, disadvantages of business partnerships often centered on relations between partners. Relations can deteriorate if the business does not do well, or if one partner is less honest or reliable or hard working than the other partners.

❖ There can be disagreement between partners on what direction the firm should take in achieving its objectives. Any unsettled disagreement between partners can threatened the existence of the firm.

❖ One of the disadvantages of partnership business is problem arising if one partner wishes to take back all or part of the capital he or she invested in the business or wishes to leave the business or if one of the partners dies. To avoid this type of problems in partnership business, before they arise. It's of paramount importance to stipulate how disputes will be solved in partnership agreement.

❖ In a partnership business, there is equal liability of each partner for losses and debts. Each partner has an unlimited personal liability, which means all the partners are responsible for any bad business dealings another partner enters into. Every decision one partner makes has potential consequences for another partner's personal assets and finances such as bank accounts, cars and houses.

❖ In a partnership business, Partners have less autonomy and equal decision-making power. Any decisions made must be jointly acceptable by the partners. This will depend on the agreement stipulated in the partnership agreement.

Registration of a Partnership Firm

Registration of a partnership firm is the same process as the registration of a sole-owner business. Both sole-owner business and a partnership business will have to provide particulars of the business owners to the Registrar of Business Names.

Limited Liability Company (LLC)

Limited Liability Company is commonly called limited company or simply LLC or company. An LLC is formed by a process called incorporation and combines the benefits of a corporation and a partnership. It provides a degree of personal liability protection while allowing for flexible management and tax benefits. LLCs are owned by members who have limited liability, meaning their personal assets are generally protected.

The capital and ownership of an LLC are divided into a number of units which are called shares or stock in some countries. A person can become a shareholder or stockholder in an LLC by investing in it and contribute towards its capital, by buying some of its shares.

Shares

Shares represent units of ownership in a company. It is exchange for money an investor paid into the company in return for a share. The person who invested in a company is issued a share certificate and the person is known as a shareholder. The share certificate is proof that he or she is the holder of a stipulated quantity of the company shares.

The quantity and value of shares are based on the following factors:

❖ *the value of capital it needs – which is known as its share capital and*
❖ *the number of different shareholders there might be.*

A company can issue shares without worrying about rules, as there is no fixed rule on number of shares or on their issued value. A company that needs a share capital of $50,000 could have 100 shares of an issued value of $500 each or 1000 shares of $50 each, or 50,000 shares of $1 each, and so on as there is no fixed rule on the number of shares. In some cases, where the number of shareholders is 2 or 3, the number of shares can be of a high value each. But, if the shareholders are to be many, more shares will be needed with relatively low value.

Shareholders

A shareholder is a person, company or institution that owns shares in a company's shares or stocks and will share in the profits made by the company in proportion to the quantity of its shares he or she holds. The amount paid per share held is called a dividend. A company shareholder can hold as little as one share. When a company loses money, the share price invariably drops, which can cause shareholders to lose money.

A shareholder as an investor in a company does not necessarily participate in the day to day running of the company. An investor who invested in a company by buying some of its shares might reap the benefits of the company's success which comes in the form of increased stock valuation or financial rewards or profits distributed as dividends.

In a small company, a single shareholder who owns and controls more than 50% of the company's outstanding shares is known as the majority shareholder. This type of shareholder is often company founder and will be involved in the day to day running of the business. In some cases, those who hold less than 50% of a company's stock are known as minority shareholders. In addition to receiving a dividend or reap the benefits of the business's success which comes in the form of financial rewards, a shareholder also has the right to vote on key corporate matters, such as naming board directors, and can vote on critical matters by proxy, either through mail-in ballots or online voting platforms if they're unable to attend voting meetings in person.

Each share gives one vote. If an investor in a company holds 100 shares, he or she will have 100 votes. If the investor holds 1000 shares, he or she will have 1,000 votes, and so on. The votes can be cast at general meetings of shareholders. In accordance to law, there must be at least one such meeting call an Annual General Meeting each financial year. Shareholders who are unable to attend the Annual General Meetings in person can vote by proxy, either through mail-in ballots or online voting platforms.

The followings are critical matters that can be voted upon and decided upon at meetings of shareholders:-

❖ The policies of the company. The shareholders of a company must agree to any major changes in its policies.

❖ The management of the company. In big companies, the shareholders elect the company board of directors to run the business on their behalf and manage their investment. In small companies, the directors are also the shareholders.

❖ The dividend. Shareholders receive financial rewards which is payable from profit, if any, made by the company during a particular financial year. In some case, dividend is usually paid to shareholders after the end of the financial or trading year.

In some cases, a vote might be the best way of settling issues should shareholders disagree on a proposition such as change of policy or the election of a company director or the amount of dividend raise at a meeting. The most votes cast the majority for or against wins the vote.

In small company, where the shareholders are two or three, there needs for concession if and when disagreement occur.

The Advantages of Limited Liability and Incorporation

Limited liability companies have favorable advantages over unlimited business ownership such as sole-proprietorship and partnership. The purpose of limited liability is to promote entrepreneurship, investment, and overall economic growth. Limited liability offers a number of notable advantages for business owners, investors and promotes entrepreneurship, investment, and overall economic growth.

The following are advantages of limited liability and incorporation:-

❖ The process of forming a new company is called formation. The new company must be registered with the appropriate government agency often known as Registrar of Companies. After the company has been registered or incorporated – the company becomes a separate, legal entity from its owner/owners. This safeguards the owner's personal assets from the debts and liabilities of the company. A limited liability company as 'an individual' may legally own assets, enter into contract, take other actions, and be responsible for its own financial issues.

❖ A limited liability entity is able to more easily raise finance for the purchase of working assets, for growth and for the other purposes by way of issuing shares to shareholders, than it is for a sole-proprietorship or for partnership business.

❖ Limited liability exists to protect personal assets of business owner/owners by blocking creditors going directly for the owner's personal assets such as property, vehicles, bank accounts, investments, etc.). This allows business owners and directors to make some calculated financial risks without fear of the potential consequences it could bring upon their personal and home life.

❖ Limited liability will Increase investor(s) confidence in investing in a company with limited liability as their obligation for any debts of the company is limited to the amount which they invested in the business; the investor(s) cannot be called upon to pay any more. This can make finding investment and outside funding significantly easier, potentially hugely beneficial to the future of the company.

❖ The death or retirement of a shareholder or director does not affect the existence of a limited liability company as a business. This not the case for sole-proprietorship and partnership business. The death or retirement of sole proprietorship and partnership business will affects the existence of both businesses respectively.

❖ The transfer of shares from one person to another does not necessarily affect the management of a company, as it does in a partnership business.

❖ The name: LIMITED LIABILITY is the most important advantage of this structure of business. Limited liability means that an investor who buys shares in a company and the company fails can lose no more than the amount of money which he or she agreed to invest for those shares. The sole-proprietor of an unincorporated business and the partner-owners in an unincorporated partnership firm, have unlimited liability for the debts of their respective business should it fail, and they can be called upon personally to pay those debts.

Corporation:

A corporation is a separate legal entity from its owners, known as shareholders. This structure offers the greatest level of liability protection, as the owners' personal assets are typically shielded from the business's debts. Corporations have a more complex structure, with shareholders, directors, and officers responsible for decision-making and management.

Choosing the right ownership structure for your business involves considering factors such as liability, taxation, management style, and growth potential. It is advisable to consult with legal and financial professionals to ensure you make an informed decision.

In the next section, we will delve deeper into each ownership structure, examining their advantages, disadvantages, and suitable business contexts. Stay tuned for valuable insights that will help you navigate the world of business ownership.

Private Companies

In some countries, there are two types of corporations (limited companies); private companies and public companies. A private company is a business entity held under private ownership and whose securities do not trade on public markets. Compare to public company. Private companies are the most popular form of corporation. But many of them are relatively small businesses and can be structured as sole proprietorships, partnerships or corporations. Many sole-proprietorships and partners change their businesses by incorporation into limited companies, to themselves the important protection of limited liability. For example, Jerome and Mukasa might well decide to forma limited liability company instead of forming a partnership business.

In some countries, a private limited company may be formed by 1 or 2 people, considering the limit imposed by law on the maximum number of shareholders there may be, and restrictions on the right of shareholders to transfer or sell the share they hold. For example, if Jerome is a shareholder and wants to sell all or some of his shares he might have to offer them to other shareholders first; if any of the shareholders do not want to buy the shares, Jerome may sell the shares to another person outside the company.

Formation and Incorporation

Company formation is the process of incorporating (registering) a business in the form of a limited company. When a company is registered, it becomes a separate legal entity; a 'person' that is completely distinct from its owners and responsible for its own finances, assets, and liabilities.

In many countries around the globe companies have to operate in accordance with documents called the Memorandum and Articles of Association, legal documents signed by all the shareholders or guarantors agreeing to formation of the company and; rules about running the company agreed by the shareholders or guarantors, directors and the company. These set out the activities in which the company will be involved.

In some countries, the process of registration is expensive due to charges on stamp duty and other form of taxes, and these charges will depend on the value of the capital of a company. The financial standing of those forming the company might be required, and restrictions on names of companies might be stricter than registration of business name.

The word "Limited" is often abbreviated to "Ltd" in some countries, and must be included as part of a company name; *for example, Jerome & Mukasa Hardware Ltd.* And, in some countries, a private company must include the word "Private" either the full name or an abbreviation such as "Pty" or "Pvt. 51

Share Held by Proxy

A shareholder proxy is a person who is appointed to stand in for a shareholder. In some countries, company regulation requires two or three persons to be the first shareholders of a new company. For example, in a situation whereby Jerome wish to be the sole-shareholder of a limited company, what Jerome can do, is to appoint a spouse or his lawyer to hold some shares. The spouse or the lawyer would sign a legal document stating that the shares the shares really belongs to Jerome and are being held on behalf of Jerome, and that the proxy cannot gain from or sell the shares without approval and agreement from Jerome

A proxy can act as an agent legally authorized to act on behalf of another party. If the shareholder cannot attend, a formal power of attorney document may be required to provide the permissions to complete certain actions. The shareholder signs a power of attorney and extends official authorization to the designated individual to vote on behalf of the stated shareholder at the annual meeting

Staying in Control

Limited liability can help to reduce the financial risk of a business, and also give a certain peace of mind to its owners. The following situations can pose danger to owner(s) of a limited liability company: =

❖ Lack of enough funds, or the ability to raise enough capital.
❖ The owner(s) lacking the require skill may have to depend on the skill of others to achieve the company objectives.

In general, a new business person might consider including one or more people into a new company as shareholders. A limited company might be the most satisfactory answer for the new business person. It is important to think beforehand the type of business to be established and the type of ownership.

Practical Example: C

Karen Mathews wishes to form a company to make and market a product which she has invented. Her funds forecast indicates that eventually the company will need capital $100, 000, of which $60,000 will be needed to start with. She can raise only $30,000 herself, but she has secured the "backing" of a Mr. Ibrahim who, although not interested in running the business, likes the product and her business plan. He agrees to invest $30,000 in the new company by buying shares in it to that value.

The two of them form a company called "Day & Night Stores Ltd" with a total 'share capital' of $100,000, made up of 10,000 shares of $10 each. They agree that Karen will be managing director; Mr. Ibrahim will be a director, but he will not be involved in running the business.

In the situation described, to begin with only 6,000 shares need be "issued" (sold or allocated): 3,000 to Karen for her $30,000 and 3,000 to Mr. Ibrahim for his $30,000. The 'issued share capital' of the company is therefore $60,000, whilst its 'unissued share capital' is $40,000 (making a total share capital of $100,000). When the company needs more issued capital to expand, it might be possible to sell some of the "unissued shares" to other people or organizations. By then, Karen might herself be able to afford to buy more.

To retain control or the 'controlling interest' in the company, Karen needs to hold more than 50% - half – of the shares, she can "win" any vote which might be have to be held at a shareholders' meeting. Control gives many advantages, and so it should not be given up lightly. Therefore, from the 6,000 shares first issued, it would be best for Karen if she could buy and hold 3,060 shares (51% of 6,000 issued) and let Mr. Ibrahim have 2,940 (49%). But Mr. Ibrahim, who is "putting up" a large sum of money, and who will not be involved in actually running the business, might insist on having the full 3,000 (50%) so that there is "parity" between them that is "50-50".

If the situation was that Karen could not raise her $30,000, she might have to hold fewer shares than Mr. Ibrahim, who would then have "control". He could still let her manage the company (as managing director) but he could have most "say" in policy matters, in deciding who might or might not also be elected a director, on dividends (if any) to be paid, and so on.

Unseen Problems of the Lack of Control
To continue the practical example of "Day & Night Stores Ltd"

After running for a while, the company needed $20,000 more capital, which could be raised by selling 2,000 more shares (leaving 2,000 only still "unissued". Karen cannot raise $20,000, and Mr. Ibrahim declines to invest more. They approach a Mr. Tom, who agrees to buy 2,000 shares for $20,000. He wishes to take no part in running the business, but wants to be a director.

Karen might feel that she is still "secure" because there is still more or less parity between the three. But that might not remain the case. As managing director Karen is in charge of the day to day running of the business. But that does not give her complete "freedom" to do as she wishes, especially with money invested by others. She has obligations to the other shareholders.

For example, say that Mr. Ibrahim and Mr. Tom feel she is spending unwisely the company's money (much of which they invested in it). If she would not listen to their objections, they could – quite legally – vote against her at a shareholders' meeting (in this case of just the three of them). Between them Mr. Ibrahim and Mr. Tom have 5,000 shares (that is, 5,000 votes), whilst Karen has only 3,000 shares (and votes). So they could "out vote" her, and require her to take action or to direct the company in a way she might not wish to do.

They could even – if they thought it necessary – at a meeting of shareholders vote to replace her as managing director and put someone else in her place. Karen might not be able to challenge that in law, and could even be voted off the board and even out of management entirely!

Such "unseen dangers" in losing control of a business through lack of financial resources (or for some other reason) must never be overlooked. There might, of course, be no alternative in some cases to "surrendering" control: but the business person concerned should think long and hard before taking such a step. It might well be worthwhile seeking the advice of a lawyer who specializes in company matters, or a business consultant. A mutually acceptable agreement between the parties might be possible, for example to allow the business person to buy some or all of the shares held by the backer(s) – probably at a "premium" (increased price) – at some future time.

Franchises

A franchise is often attractive to new business people because it offers the chance to run a business with relatively little capital, which it might be impossible to run "independently". A franchise might be gained by a limited company, or in some cases by a sole=owner or by a partnership.

Some franchising has been in existence for a long time; for example petrol or gas stations, and motor vehicle distributors. Today it extends to restaurants and other types of eating-places, printing, motor vehicle exhaust and tyre fitting and servicing, and "standard" repairs, home and carpet cleaning, and many other activities.

In a simplified way, this is how franchising works:
Over a number of years, Karen's company, "Day & Night Stores Ltd", grows and extends the range of products it manufactures. Its products are well-known and the "brand name" of "Day & Night Stores Ltd" is easily identifiable. In order to grow – to expand – and to increase profits made by the business, it might be necessary to open numerous "outlets" (shops or stores). But the owners of "Day & Night Stores Ltd" (who might or might not still include Karen) might not wish to become involved in establishing and running many outlets. Instead, other people – as individuals and/or as groups – are found who are willing to establish and run those outlets – as "franchisees" – under the "brand

name" of "Day & Night Stores Ltd" but as "semi-independent" businesses under "franchise agreements"

The owner of a franchise – the owner(s) of the "original" business – "Day & Night Stores Ltd" in this example – is called the 'franchiser'. The franchiser supplies each franchisee with a well-known "brand name", certain products and/or equipment, general services (such as advertising and publicity), know-how and training, and any contacts made in the franchisee's allocated "territory".

Franchise agreements vary, but in general the franchisee business has to pay a set fee plus a proportion of its income to the franchiser. From the point of view of the franchiser, growth can be achieved – and savings often made due to increased production or bulk buying – without heavy capital layout, or the need to manage (and staff) numerous outlets.

From the franchisee's point of view, a profitable business can be run, and experience gained, with a relatively modest capital outlay. To a certain extent risk is reduced because the brand name is already established and "known". However, the location of a particular franchiser business and the "market" are important.

Your Decision

We have now given you information about different types of business ownership, and the possible advantages and disadvantages of each type. You need to consider carefully – based on your own particular circumstances and financial position – which is most likely to be the best type of ownership for the business you are running, or which you propose to start or take over – now or at a later date.

It is most important, however, that you make your decision based on all the facts available to you at the time, and with consideration of the forecasts of the likely future position, as set out in your business plan.

Trade Licenses

In addition to registration, in many countries, businesses (sometimes only those dealing in certain products or commodities) might have to apply for and secure local or national licenses to operate. This is a matter which you need to look into (perhaps at your town or city hall or other local government office) because it might be illegal to operate without a license. Failure to comply with local or national regulations might result in the imposition of a penalty – such as a fine – on your business or on you personally and possibly even the suspension of your business operations.

CHAPTER QUESTIONS TWO – CHAPTER 2

> *Recommended Answers to the Questions-against which you may compare your answers-are in the Appendix after the end of this Chapter. The maximum mark which may be awarded for each Question appears in brackets at the end of the Question.*

No.1. Describe briefly the three main types of business ownership, and specify which you would prefer for your business, and why. (maximum 40 marks)

No.2. (a) What advantages might there be to a new business person in securing a "franchise" to run a business in a particular "territory"? (maximum 20 marks)

(b) What is the importance of keeping "control" over your business? How can that be done in a limited liability company? (maximum 20 marks)

No.3. Place a tick in the box against the **one correct** statement in each set.

(a) Unlimited personal liability of a business owner means that:
1. ☐ the personal possessions of its owner can be seized and sold to raise money to pay the debts of the business.
2. ☐ he or she has far too many obligations to fulfill.
3. ☐ he or she has invested very little money in the business..
4. ☐ there is nothing to stop it expanding to become very large.

(b) An entrepreneur is a person:
1. ☐ who undertakes a commercial or business venture, often at personal or financial risk.
2. ☐ who runs a business in Chile.
3. ☐ who runs the simplest and safest type of business.
4. ☐ who has sufficient capital to start and run a business without needing to borrow money from a bank.

(c) The "factors of production" are:
1.☐ the place in which goods are manufactured.
2.☐ business people who sell manufactured goods.
3.☐ land, labour and capital.
4.☐ the materials and components which are needed in order to be able to produce a finished product ready for sale.

(d) A person who hold shares in a company "by proxy":
1.☐ is the legal owner of those shares..
2.☐ holds them on behalf of another person, who is their real owner.
3.☐ has to be a director of that company.
4.☐ has control of the company and can direct its activities.

(e) A sole-owner business:
1.☐ is engaged in making components for shoes and boots.
2.☐ is involved in finishing.
3.☐ is owned by just one person.
4.☐ is involved in raising money for charities.

No.4. Place a tick in the box against the one correct statement in each set.
(a) In business, a "profit" is:
1.☐ a religious person who foretells the future.
2.☐ the amount of income received by a business.
3.☐ a return on the capital invested in a business.
4.☐ the total amount of the expenses paid by a business.

(b) A partnership business is owned by:
1.☐ two or more people working together with the common goal of profit.
2.☐ a husband and a wife.
3.☐ just one person working on his or her own.
4.☐ its directors.

(c) It is most important that any business:
1.☐ is registered with the appropriate authority in the country.
2.☐ is always owned by two or more people.
3.☐ has the word "limited" in its name.
4.☐ is incorporated.

(d) A company's share capital:
1.☐ need to be issued in full when it is first started.
2.☐ need not all be issued at one time.
3.☐ should be raised from loans.
4.☐ should always be made up of 1,000 shares.

(e) It is important that a partnership firm:
1.☐ divides profits made equally between its partners.
2.☐ operates in accordance with a signed "partnership agreement".
3.☐ has working as well as non-working partners.
4.☐ admits new partners at regular intervals to bring in new ideas.

(2 marks for a statement correctly ticked – maximum 20

Chapter 3
LOCATION OF BUSINESSES

Introduction

The premises where a business is operated from is called its Location. Choosing the right location for your business is a critical decision that can greatly impact its success. With so many factors to consider, it can be overwhelming to determine where best to establish your company. However, by carefully evaluating key factors and conducting thorough research, you can make an informed decision that aligns with your business goals. In this chapter, we will explore the factors to consider when locating a business and provide valuable insights to help you determine the optimal location for your venture.

Factors to consider when locating a business:-

- *The type of business to startup.*
- *The types or natures of the products the business will produce and/or sell.*
- *The type of market the business will compete.*
- *The type of customers the business will target.*
- *The financial status of the business owner(s).*
- *Suitability and cost of the business premises.*

Production

Production is a fundamental concept in the world of business and economics. It refers to the process of creating goods or services through various stages of transformation. Simply put, production is the act of combining resources, such as labor, capital, and materials, to produce output that satisfies consumer demand. While the concept of production may seem straightforward, it involves complex decision-making, coordination, and optimization. This chapter dives deeper into the concept of production, its importance in the economy, and the different types and factors of production. Read on to gain a comprehensive understanding of what production truly entails.

Types of Businesses

We can also consider the following types of businesses based on their activities.

✓ **Industrial**

The term **"industrial"** is often used to describe anything related to manufacturing or producing goods on a large scale. However, the concept of industrial goes beyond just factories and production lines. It encompasses a wide range of sectors and activities, from energy and transportation to construction and infrastructure development. There are many businesses of various sizes offering a wide range of activities which result of availability of different products. In this chapter, we will explore the definition of industrial and its significance in today's global economy. Whether you are a business owner, investor, or simply curious about the inner workings of various industries, this chapter will provide you with a comprehensive understanding of what industrial truly means, ***the type of activities in which they are involved as outlined below:***

- **Extractive Industrial:** This refers to the process of extracting natural resources from the earth for commercial use. It encompasses industries such as mining, oil and gas extraction, and forestry. Extractive industries play a vital role in providing raw materials for various sectors of the economy, including manufacturing and energy production. However, these industries also raise concerns regarding environmental impact, social responsibility, and sustainable practices. This chapter explores the concept of extractive industrial and its significance in modern society.

- **Processing or Refining Industrial:** In the industrial sector, there are several key processes that play a crucial role in transforming raw materials into finished products. Two of these fundamental processes are processing and refining. Both processing and refining are integral parts of the industrial production chain. *For example, crude oil is refined into petrol, diesel to fuel machinery and motor vehicles.*

- **Manufacturing:** Manufacturing is a fundamental aspect of the industrial sector, encompassing the processes involved in transforming raw materials into finished goods. It is a complex and multifaceted industry that plays a crucial role in the global economy. From automobile production to food processing, manufacturing spans a wide range of sectors and products.

- **Construction Industrial:** Construction is a vast and complex industry that encompasses the planning, designing, and building of structures, as well as the maintenance and repair of existing ones. Within this industry, there are various sectors and sub-sectors, each with its own set of challenges and requirements.

  One such sector is construction industrial, which focuses on large scale projects such as industrial facilities, power plants, and infrastructure.

Commercial

In the business world, the term **"commercial"** is often used to describe activities and transactions that involve the buying and selling of goods and services. However, the concept of commercial extends beyond just buying and selling. It encompasses a wide range of activities, including marketing, advertising, finance, and law.

Understanding what is considered **"commercial"** and how it impacts businesses and consumers is essential for anyone involved in the business world. In this chapter, we will explore the meaning and significance of commercial, its various aspects and the *type of activities in which they are involved as outlined below:*

✓ **Trading and Distribution**

Trading and distribution are two fundamental components of the global supply chain. Both are crucial in getting goods from manufacturers to consumers, ensuring the availability and accessibility of products in the market. While these terms are often used interchangeably, they have distinct roles and responsibilities within the distribution channel. This chapter aims to explore the definitions and nuances of trading and distribution, as well as their significance in the world of business. Whether you are an aspiring entrepreneur or simply curious about the inner workings of the market, this chapter will provide valuable insights into the essential concepts of trading and distribution, and the *type of activities in which they are involved as broadly categorized below:*

➢ **Domestic Trade**

This type of trade refers to the buying and selling of goods and services within a country's own borders. It involves transactions between individuals, businesses, and government entities, and plays a crucial role in the overall economic development of a nation. Understanding the concept and dynamics of domestic trade is essential for businesses and policymakers alike, as it impacts factors such as employment, production, and economic growth. In this chapter, we will delve deeper into the world of domestic trade, exploring its definition, importance, and key characteristics *as broadly categorized below:*

- **Retailers:** In the world of business and commerce, retailers play a crucial role in the distribution of goods to the end consumer. But what exactly are retailers and what do they do? In simplest terms, retailers are businesses or individuals who purchase products from wholesalers or manufacturers and sell them directly to consumers. They operate in a variety of industries, from clothing to electronics to groceries. Retailers serve as the middleman between suppliers and consumers, ensuring that products are available and accessible to the public.

- **Large – scale stores:** Large-scale stores, also known as big-box retailers or superstores or supermarkets, are retail establishments that have massive purchasing power offering a wide selection of products in a single location. These stores are characterized by their extensive floor space and vast inventory, allowing them to cater to a diverse range of consumer needs. Large-scale stores have become increasingly popular in recent years, particularly due to their ability to offer competitive pricing and a one-stop shopping experience.

- **Wholesalers:** Wholesalers play a crucial role in the supply chain, connecting manufacturers and retailers by purchasing goods in large quantities and selling them to smaller businesses. They serve as intermediaries, helping to distribute products efficiently and effectively. Wholesalers provide a range of services, including warehousing, inventory management, and transportation. This chapter explores the role of wholesalers in the business world and discusses their importance in modern commerce. Whether you are a manufacturer or a retailer, understanding wholesalers and their functions is essential for success in today's competitive market.

> ### International Trade

This type of trade plays a crucial role in the global economy, facilitating the exchange of goods and services between countries. It involves the import and export of products and services across borders, and is essential for economic growth and development. Understanding the concept of international trade is important for businesses, policymakers, and individuals alike, as it influences factors such as employment, investment, and economic stability. This chapter provides an overview of what international trade are, its significance, and the various factors that contribute to its success. Whether you are a student, a business owner, or simply interested in global economics, this chapter will provide valuable insights into the world of international trade including the main types of international trade, *as broadly outlined below:-*

- **Export:** This type of international trade plays a crucial role in international trade, contributing significantly to the economic growth and development of nations. It involves the sale and shipment of goods or services from one country to another, typically to meet the demand of foreign markets. Understanding the concept of export and its importance in global commerce is essential for businesses and individuals seeking to expand their reach beyond domestic borders. This chapter provides a comprehensive overview of export, including its definition, processes, and benefits, to help you navigate the world of international trade successfully.

- **Import:** This type of international trade plays a crucial role in international trade, contributing to the economy and affecting the prices and availability of goods. But what exactly is import? It refers to the act of bringing goods or services into a country from abroad for the purpose of sale or use. From raw materials and components used in manufacturing to finished products and consumer goods, imports have a significant impact on various sectors of the economy.

- **Entréport:** This is a term that is gaining traction in the business world, yet many people are still unfamiliar with its meaning and significance. In short, entréport refers to a specific type of business that acts as both an entry point and a gateway for entrepreneurs. This concept combines the idea of an entry point or access point with the notion of a seaport or airport, symbolizing the potential for growth, expansion, and global connections that these businesses offer.

For example, a trader imports goods from abroad into his or her country without repackaging or any form of processing, the goods are then re-exported to other countries. In this circle, the trader acts as both the exporter and importer at the same time.

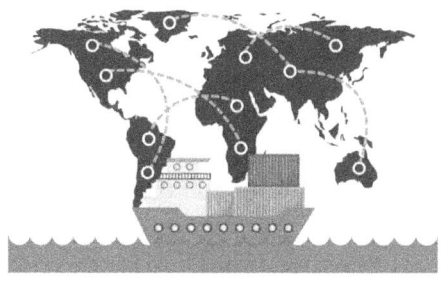

Services Providing

In the world of business, there are many different types of industries and sectors. One such sector is the services providing business, which encompasses a wide range of businesses that offer services rather than physical products. From consulting firms to marketing agencies to IT support companies, the services providing business sector plays a crucial role in the economy. In this chapter, we will explore what exactly a services providing business is and how it operates. Whether you are considering starting your own services providing business or simply want to learn more about this sector, this chapter is right for you.

The followings are major type of businesses involved in services providing industrial.

- **Accountancy:** Accountancy is a fundamental aspect of business operations that plays a crucial role in financial decision-making and ensuring the integrity and accuracy of financial records. It encompasses a wide range of activities, including recording, analyzing, interpreting, and reporting financial information. Accountants use their expertise and knowledge to help businesses navigate complex financial regulations, manage tax obligations, and optimize financial performance. In this blog, we will explore the ins and outs of accountancy, its importance in the business world, and the skills required to excel in this profession. Whether you are a business owner, aspiring accountant, or simply curious about the field, this blog will provide you with a comprehensive understanding of accountancy.

- **Accommodation and Catering:** Accommodation refers to the provision of lodging or housing for travelers, whether it is in hotels, resorts, or vacation rentals. Catering, on the other hand, involves providing food and beverage services for events or functions, such as weddings, business conferences, or private parties. Both accommodation and catering are crucial aspects of ensuring a positive and enjoyable experience for guests.

- **Banking and Finance:** Banking and finance are two intertwined sectors that play a crucial role in the global economy. **Banking** refers to the activities conducted by financial institutions, such as banks, to provide services to individuals, businesses, and governments. **Finance**, on the other hand, encompasses the management of money and assets, including investments, lending, and financial planning. Together, **banking and finance** form the foundation of our modern financial system, facilitating economic growth and stability.

- **Insurance:** Insurance plays a crucial role in our lives, providing protection and financial security in the face of unexpected events. But what exactly is insurance? It is a contract between an individual or organization and an insurance company, where the insured pays a premium in exchange for the promise of compensation in the event of a covered loss. Insurance is a complex industry with various types of coverage available to protect against risks such as property damage, accidents, illness, and more.

- **Maintenance and Repair:** Maintenance and repair are essential aspects of ensuring the longevity and functionality of various systems and equipment. From household appliances to complex industrial machinery, every system requires regular maintenance to prevent problems and repair services when issues arise. Maintenance involves regular checks, inspections, and necessary adjustments to keep the system in optimal condition, while repair involves fixing any malfunctions or damages.

- **Transportation:** Transportation is a fundamental aspect of modern society, facilitating the movement of people and goods from one place to another. It plays a crucial role in the functioning of economies, enabling trade, tourism, and the access to essential services. Transport systems have evolved significantly over time, adapting to new technologies, changing demographics, and societal needs.

- **Warehousing:** Warehousing is an essential component of supply chain management that plays a crucial role in the storage, handling, and distribution of goods. It refers to the process of storing and managing inventory in a designated facility, known as a warehouse, until it is needed for consumption or shipment. Warehousing involves various activities, such as receiving, storing, picking, packing, and shipping goods, as well as inventory control and record-keeping.

Consumers and Corporate Buyers

There are two main classes of buyers who buys products businesses sell. These classes of buyers are the end-user, known as consumers and, the corporate buyers. Buyers can be referred by different terms such as; *purchasers, customers, clients, regular, patrons, passengers, guests, subscribers, visitors, travellers, viewers, spectators, fans,* and so on by different businesses.

- **Consumers:** In the world of marketing and business, understanding consumer behavior is crucial for success. After all, consumers are the ones who ultimately decide whether or not to purchase a product or service. But what exactly is consumer buying behavior? Consumer buying behavior refers to the process by which individuals search for, select, purchase, and use goods and services to satisfy their needs and desires. It involves complex factors such as psychological, social, and cultural influences that shape consumers' decision-making processes.

- **Corporate Buyers:** Corporate buyers play a critical role in the purchasing process of goods and services for businesses. These professionals are responsible for selecting the suppliers and negotiating contracts that meet the needs of their organizations. They are tasked with evaluating and sourcing the best products and services at the most competitive prices, all while ensuring quality and reliability.

   ✓ **Natures of Products We Buy**

Products can be divided into goods and services and can each be further subdivided into two groups below:-

'necessities' or **'essentials'** and **'luxuries'** or **'nonessentials'**

- **Necessities and Luxuries:** In today's consumer-driven society, it can be easy to lose sight of the distinction between what is truly essential and what is considered a luxury. The line between necessities and luxuries has become increasingly blurred, with the availability of a wide range of products and services at our fingertips. However, understanding the difference between the two is crucial for making informed purchasing decisions and managing our finances effectively. Any products which consumers buy which are not essential, but add to the quality and comfort of life, might be considered to be nonessentials, and thus luxuries. For example, to a laborer a smartphone would be luxury, but to a tech engineer in the same location or country a smartphone might be very essential, as he could not perform his work effectively if he or she did not have access to the internet to download device software.

Necessities are basic and staple items which people need. In general, people know what necessity items they need and can afford, and do not need to be persuaded to buy. They will simply ask shop assistants for what they want, or will collect the items from, say, supermarket shelves, and take them to a check-out point where they will pay. Salesmanship is not needed in such circumstances – unless consumers have a choice of similar products, in which case some selling skill might be needed to persuade them to buy one make or brand rather than another.

Luxuries are items which consumers may not really need, but which they can afford to buy, to make their lives more comfortable and enjoyable. There is often a fairly wide range of such nonessential items available, but between which consumers must select, because their spending power is limited. Skillful salesmanship is needed to persuade consumers to spend their money on certain types of products instead of other types, and on specific products instead of on similar ones sold by competitors.

- **Choice Factor Products:** This refers to a specific line of goods that have been carefully curated and selected based on their quality, value, and customer satisfaction. These products are chosen by experts in the industry who are dedicated to providing consumers with the best options available. Whether it's in the realm of electronics, home goods, or fashion, Choice Factor Products are known for their exceptional standards and reliability.

When consumers have a **choice** of makes or brand of necessity items each manufacturer or producer tries to persuade consumers to purchase their products, rather than those of competitors.

- **Essentials and Nonessentials:** In the world of business and consumerism, it is essential to understand the distinction between **essential and nonessential** products. Essential products are those that are necessary for everyday life and are considered basic needs, such as food, water, and shelter.

Nonessential products, on the other hand, are luxury items or goods that are not required for survival. This distinction becomes particularly relevant during times of crisis or economic downturn, as consumer behavior and spending habits often shift.

Important services such as electricity, telecommunications, banking, transport and so on are essential for the success of most business, and adequate insurance cover is also essential if they are to be able to continue to operate in the event of losses due to fire, theft, flood, accidents, and so on. Modern office equipment such as electronic calculators, photocopies, computers, fax machines, and so on are essential to businesses of various sizes.

✓ The Market for the Products

Understanding the market for products is a crucial aspect of any business strategy. It is essential to identify and analyze the target market to ensure that products are developed, promoted, and distributed effectively. The market for products refers to the specific group of consumers or businesses that are likely to have an interest in purchasing a particular product.

By understanding the market for products, businesses can tailor their marketing efforts, pricing strategies, and product development to meet the needs and preferences of their target customers. This article explores the concept of the market for products and its importance in strategic decision-making.

✓ Competition

Competition is a fundamental concept in the world of business. It refers to the rivalry between companies that offer similar products or services and are vying for the same customers. In a competitive business environment, companies must constantly strive to differentiate themselves and gain a competitive advantage over their rivals. This can be achieved through various means, such as offering superior products, providing better customer service, or implementing more efficient business processes. Understanding the concept of competition is crucial for businesses to thrive in today's competitive market landscape. In this article, we will explore what competition is, its significance in the business world, and how companies can navigate and leverage competition to achieve success.

✓ The Classes of Customers

In the world of business, understanding your customers is key to success. Identifying and categorizing your customers into different groups or segments allows you to tailor your marketing strategies and provide personalized experiences. One commonly used method of segmentation is classifying customers based on their characteristics, preferences, and behaviors. This approach, known as the class of customer, helps businesses gain valuable insights into their customer base and make informed decisions. In this article, we will explore what exactly the class of customer is and why it is important in today's competitive market.

❖ Where to Locate a Business

Having considered all the major factors in locating a business, where do you locate your business? Several personal factors might have bearing on your choice of answers such as where you live, or where you want to work?

- **Working from Home:** In recent years, there has been a significant shift in the way people work. More and more individuals are embracing the concept of working from home, also known as remote work or telecommuting. But what exactly does it mean to work from home? Is it just lounging in pajamas all day or is it a legitimate way to maintain productivity and balance work and personal life? This article will explore the definition of working from home, its benefits and challenges, and provide tips for those considering this flexible work arrangement. So, let's dive in and discover what working from home is really all about.

- **Passing Trade:** Passing trade is a term commonly used in the business world to describe the customers who make spontaneous purchases or engage in a service without prior planning or intention. These customers typically come across a store or a business while passing by, and are enticed to make a purchase due to **attractive displays** of products for sale in their shop or showroom windows or compelling advertising. *Window displays are designed to appeal to the eyes of passers-by, to compel them to stop and look closer at items in the displays.* The concept of passing trade is especially relevant to businesses located in high foot traffic areas such as *malls, tourist destinations, or busy city centers.* Examples of passing trade include shop, stores and showrooms selling fashions, footwear, stationeries, jewellery, televisions and DVD players, electrical appliances, computers, cosmetics, and many more.

- Often the type of business dictates where it should or can be located. For example, a business which depends for its trade on passers-by must be located in a busy thoroughfare-preferably at street level-which many customers pass along every day. Shopping malls or arcades (even on upper storeys) are also suitable for such businesses. But businesses which do not depend upon, or seek, passing trade, can be located in quieter areas, away from main streets (perhaps on upper storeys of buildings). Examples are businesses which provide repair and commercial services, wholesalers, manufacturers, building and timber merchants.

A business usually needs to be located conveniently for the market for its products; that is, for people who are most likely to buy its products, and those who can afford to do so. Much depends on the natures of the products a business is selling, and on the financial status of its likely customers; that is, their demands and preferences. A launderette or laundrymat, for example, would best be located in a high-density residential area in which few people own washing machines. Such a business would not have a good market in a working or office area in which few people actually live.

Customers or clients of some businesses will find them, if they are not too inconveniently situated, and if they are situated in areas in which those people feel "comfortable". Other businesses, for example, a vocational college, can be located hundreds or thousands of kilometers from their clients, so long as there are efficient communications (post, telephones, fax, and email.)

- **Quieter Areas:** Many businesses that do not depend on passing- trade can locate their businesses on high rise building or upper storeys of buildings, or faraway from busy business areas. This types of businesses include those which provide services such as insurance agents or brokers, accountants, lawyers, tradesmen, artisans such as tailors, shoemakers, fashion designers, hairdressers, technicians such as those who repair electrical appliances, watches, radios and televisions, welders, carpenters, plumbers, and so on. Other professionals such as travel agents, estate agents, banks, microfinance and building societies need to be situated in busy business districts.

- **City Outskirts:** Most businesses such as wholesale businesses do not need to be in city central, and might be situated in city outskirts, which is quieter, and where it is possible to find large areas of storage space and uncongested access for free movement for vehicles delivering and pickup merchandises. Business dealing with building materials, forestry materials such timbers, woods, businesses in repairing and servicing motor vehicles will often be located outskirts of busy city centers where they need large working space, cheaper and easier access for road, rail or even water transportation. Some businesses locate in local councils business parks, industrial estates or trading estates located in city outskirts. Others might have their shops or stores in the city centers or in shopping malls, but have their stocks of commodities for sale stored in premises on city outskirts.

Practical Examples D: Natures of Goods

A woman who wants to set up a fruit and vegetable shop, the best location for such a trade would be a busy marketplace or a busy shopping mall frequented by housewives or different type of shoppers where competition from similar trade is not available. If the woman located in an area frequented mainly by office workers or business, her business will not survive, because those people are not the type of customers for the products of that type of business. Businesses such as those which sell office equipment, stationery, printing; travel agents, insurance agents, banking agents, those providing business and professional services, financial services, banking, employment agency, cafés and restaurants, and secretarial services. Others are businesses such as newsagents, tobacconists, confectionists, and so on. Locations such as office blocks, cinemas, sports complex will be suitable to the type of products for sale. Businesses should be located in areas in which likely customers for their products live, work or where customers frequently visit.

Practical Examples E: Classes of Customers

We must consider that natures of products relate directly to the class of customer to whom sales of goods or service are most likely to be made. Whether or not the qualities and prices of products will be considered essentials or luxuries by targeted buyers, all must be thought about very carefully. It should be carefully considered before deciding there is a market in the location for the types of products a business hoped to sell. Businesses such as jewellery, high valued household appliances, expensive furniture, television sets, DVD players, cameras, computers, cosmetics and clothing cannot sell in areas frequented mainly by people with low-incomes. In similar fashion, businesses selling cheap products would find little or no markets in areas frequented by wealthy people.

❖ High Priced Products versus Low Priced Products

Some business owners believe that it is more profitable to sell high price products than to sell lower price products. The possibility that market for high price items might be quiet small, but the profit on each unit sold might be quiet high. In similar fashion, the possibility that market for lower price items might be much larger, but the profit margin on each unit will probably be low.

Business owners hoping to attract affluent customers will normally, locate their businesses in expensive buildings, in plush areas or neighborhoods. They might decorate their premises with expensive, luxurious furnishing and decors to meet customer's expectation.

❖ What Premises are Available, and the Cost to Rent or Buy?

It is important to note that different types of businesses require different types of premises. A business located in premises in busiest areas of the city is likely to be expensive to rent or to buy. Some businesses need shops or showrooms, others need offices or storehouses, warehouses, stockyards, and others need factory sites. Some businesses are best located on ground level, whilst others can be located on upper storeys of buildings. Some businesses need large premises; others might need only small areas, like kiosks.

It might be well to admit that you will not be able to find exact type and size of premises in the most suitable location, and at the right price. You might well have to reach a "compromise" between good features and less good ones.

Research

It is wise not to select business location based on guesswork or on instinct alone. Before making any decision, it is advisable to get as much information as possible about the area which you think might be suitable for your business, even if you are familiar with the area by carrying out some **investigation and research**. It is very important that you gain a good idea of the size of the market in the general area for the products you want to sell. For example, if you were planning to open a convenience store in a particular area. It is advisable to chat to other shop owners, in the area you want to locate the convenience store or contact the local Chamber of Commerce office for accurate information.

If the location in which a business is established is found from experience to be unsuitable, it might not be easy to move it to another location. Even if that is possible, it will involve expense, and probably loss of customers.

It is therefore important to research possible locations for your business in advance, before making a final selection. A location which seems ideal might, in fact, have hidden problems, which will only be discovered by research. For example, competitors might be planning to move into the area. Or major road works (a bypass for example) might divert traffic (and customers) away from the area. On the other hand, you might learn about factors which can make a particular location more attractive than it seems. For instance, that the local council is offering low rents to encourage new businesses to its area.

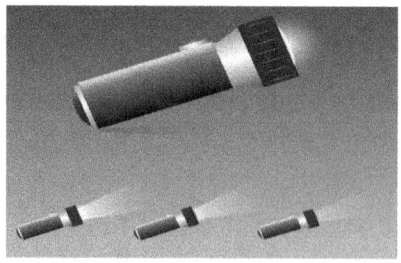

CHAPTER QUESTIONS THREE – CHAPTER 3

> *Recommended Answers to the Questions-against which you may compare your answers-are in the Appendix after the end of this Chapter. The maximum mark which may be awarded for each Question appears in brackets at the end of the Question.*

No.1. In what way does the type of business and the market for its products dictate the most suitable location for a business? (maximum 20 marks)

No.2. (a) Describe the difference between necessity products and luxury products as far as consumers are concerned? (maximum 20 marks)

(b) For what reasons should "research" be undertaken before deciding where best to locate a business? (maximum 20 marks)

No.3. Place a tick √ in the box against the **one correct** statement in each set.

(a) In business a "consumer" is:
1.☐ a customer of a café, restaurant or some other eating place.
2.☐ a person who buys products on behalf of an organization he or she owns or works for.
3.☐ a person who buys products and makes use of them, in various ways, in his or her everyday life.
4.☐ a person who buys only grocery products.

(b) When consumers have a "choice" of makes or brands:
1.☐ they buy those which taste the best to them.
2.☐ they need to be persuaded to buy the products of a certain producer or manufacturer.
3.☐ they buy only necessity items.
4.☐ they select them from supermarket.

(c) With regard to "competition" it is important to consider:
1.☐ the likely future competition as well as present competition in the area in which you might locate your business.
2.☐ whether it is a game or match your business can enter.
3.☐ the increase in numbers of customers it will bring about.
4.☐ they select them from supermarket shelves.

(d) The term "passing-trade" refers to:
1.☐ business which has been carried out in the past.
2.☐ selling products by the self-selection method, e.g. in supermarkets.
3.☐ successful and profitable business.
4.☐ people passing the premises of a business who can be attracted in.

(e) Sales of lower priced products:
1.☐ are not as profitable as selling highly priced products.
2.☐ are more profitable than selling expensive products.
3.☐ can be as profitable as sales of highly priced products.
4.☐ are not profitable if sold from large shops or stores.

No.4. Place a tick in the box against the one correct statement in each set.

(a) The final selection of premises for a business:
1.☐ might be a compromise between good features and less good ones.
2.☐ will depend on the cheapest available at the time.
3.☐ will be based on guesswork by the business person.
4.☐ will be on the advice of a friend or neighbor.

(b) Attractive window displays:
1.☐ can encourage people to enter the premises of a business to buy.
2.☐ prevent people seeing into the premises of a shop or store.
3.☐ are best in quieter back street where people have time to look.
4.☐ are only used in town or city centers.

(c) The common activities of trading and distribution businesses are:

1.☐ manufacturing products and components.
2.☐ buying and selling raw materials, components and finished goods.
3.☐ extracting materials from the land or sea.
4.☐ providing services for individuals and organizations.

(d) Wholesale businesses:

1.☐ sell products mainly to consumers in small quantities.
2.☐ are so called because they sell only complete products.
3.☐ do not allow customers to buy "on credit" without paying at once.
4.☐ buy in large quantities and resell to retailers in smaller quantities.

(e) Retailers in business are:

1.☐ people who earn their living by writing or telling stories.
2.☐ tradespeople who repair roofs and replace broken tiles.
3.☐ businesses which sell mainly in smallish quantities to consumers.
4.☐ people who make and sell articles of clothing.

(2 marks for a statement correctly ticked – maximum 20

Chapter 4
BUYING OR TAKING OVER
AN ESTABLISHED BUSINESS

Process of Acquiring an Established Business

Buying or taking over an established business refers to the process of acquiring an existing company. This can be achieved through a variety of means, such as purchasing the assets or shares of the business, entering into a merger or acquisition agreement, or assuming control through a management buyout.

There are several reasons why individuals or organizations may consider buying or taking over an existing business. For starters, it provides a quicker route to entering the market compared to starting a business from scratch. By acquiring an established business, you can benefit from its existing customer base, brand recognition, and operational infrastructure.

Additionally, taking over an existing business allows you to bypass many of the challenges and risks associated with starting a new venture. Rather than having to build a reputation and establish relationships from scratch, you can build upon the existing reputation and relationships of the acquired business.

When considering buying or taking over an existing business, it is important to conduct thorough due diligence. This includes assessing the financial health of the business, analyzing its market position, evaluating its assets and liabilities, and reviewing any legal or contractual obligations. This information will help you determine the value of the business and identify any potential risks or opportunities.

It is also crucial to have a well-developed business acquisition strategy in place. This includes determining your objectives for the acquisition, identifying the target market and industry, and establishing a budget and financing plan. Engaging professional advisors such as lawyers, accountants, and business brokers can provide valuable guidance throughout the acquisition process.

Buying or taking over an existing business can be a complex endeavor, but it offers the potential for significant rewards. With careful planning, due diligence, and strategic execution, acquiring an established business can be a beneficial step towards achieving your entrepreneurial goals. As the business being acquired is what is often known as **going concern**, there are many different reasons why a business is being acquired; *and these are some of the reasons*:-

- When a business is for sale, some of the reasons could be that an individual or a group of people is planning to establish the same type of business in the same location.

- When a new started operation in the same location, it might have to compete with the existing business. To avoid competition, buying the existing business will be harmless to both the new and the established businesses.

- Another reason is that the ownership of an established business is considering establishing another branch in other to extend the range of activities. For example, Jackie might find that she could expand her business activities by offering fashion design service for clothes, shoes and ladies handbags. Acquiring an existing fashion design service which has the necessary equipment and customers already would be helpful to her business, because she will not have to start a new business from scratch.

- If you are ever considering buying or taking over an established business as a **going concern** or secure the use of desirable premises, the best way of achieving that is to buy the business presently operating from them. You can continue with the same type of business from the premises or start a different business from the same premises.

The following factors should be included in your decision if you are thinking about buying or taking over an established business.

The factors are: - capital, ownership, the market, competition, experience and skills, and so on.

Some Business Terms

There are some businesses terms to which you need to understand before buying or taking over an established business. Some you might have come across before and some have different meanings in modern business.

- **Assets:** Assets refer to the economic resources owned or controlled by a company that provide future benefits. These can include physical assets such as buildings, equipment, and inventory, as well as intangible assets like patents, trademarks, and goodwill. The value of assets is typically measured at their historical cost, less any depreciation or impairment.

- **Debtors:** These refer to people or businesses that owe money to a business. For example, if you take out a car loan from your bank, you're the debtor and the bank is the creditor in this transaction. Money owed to a business is one of its assets.

- **Liabilities:** These are the obligations or debts that a company owes to external parties (people and/or organizations). These can include loans, accounts payable, accrued expenses, and other financial obligations. Like assets, liabilities are recorded at their historical cost, which is the amount owed at the time of acquisition.

- **Creditors:** These are individuals and/or businesses that have lent money to another individual or entity. They typically charge interest to the borrowers and /or debtors. For example, a bank lending money to a person and/or businesses is the creditor. If a person or a business has a bank overdraft, the bank is the creditors.

- **Credit:** This term is different from creditor. Credit is the ability of a customer to obtain goods or services before payment is made or received at a later date.

- ✓ If a person or a business buys goods '**on credit'**, without paying for them at once, it owes a **debt** of their value, which is a **liability**. The person or business, to whom the money is still owed for goods or services, is a **creditor** of the business.

- ✓ If a person or a business sells goods '**on credit'**, without receiving payment for them at once, a **debt** of their value is owned to it, the debt is an **asset**. The person or business, who owes the money to the business for goods or services, is a **debtor** of that business.

- **Stock:** In some countries stock is called **Inventory**. Stocks or inventory are asset of the business. This term refers to all the items, goods, merchandise, and materials held by a business for resale in the market to earn a profit.

- **Accounts:** This term refers to record or statement of financial expenditure , transactions and exchange of money which a business has with other parties (persons and/or organizations).

Why the Business is For Sale

The decision to put a business up for sale can stem from a variety of factors, and gaining a clear understanding of why a business is on the market is essential before considering an acquisition. There are several common reasons why a business may be for sale, each with its own set of implications and considerations.

One common reason is **retirement**. Many business owners choose to sell their businesses as they approach retirement age, looking to transition into a new phase of life and secure financial stability for the future. In these cases, the business is often well-established and has a solid track record, making it an attractive opportunity for potential buyers.

Another reason for selling a business is a **strategic decision** by the owner. Businesses may be sold as part of a larger corporate strategy to focus on core operations or divest non-core assets. This could be due to market changes, shifts in industry dynamics, or a desire to reallocate resources to other ventures. In these instances, the business may still be in good standing, but the owner has determined that it is no longer aligned with their long-term goals.

Financial struggles can also lead to a business being put up for sale. In some cases, businesses may face challenges, such as declining revenue, increasing costs, or a lack of profitability, that make it difficult to continue operations. Selling the business can be a way to recoup some of the investment and minimize financial losses.

Its Accounts

Normally, the business owner (s) will be able to produce financial records and other important documents showing the volume of business done, and if the business is profitable or not by including the final accounts covering one or more years. It is important to understand what final accounts of any business entails, as final account will not give information about the present financial position of the business, but financial position about a past or historical position of the business. In some cases, final accounts might not be a 'true' lead to the position of the business at the time you are considering buying or taking over the business.

Additionally, **personal factors** can play a role in the decision to sell a business. Health issues, family circumstances, or other personal considerations may make it necessary for an owner to exit their business. While these situations can be more challenging for potential buyers to evaluate, they may present unique opportunities for those with the expertise and resources to overcome any obstacles.

Understanding why a business is for sale is crucial in determining whether it is a viable investment opportunity. By conducting thorough due diligence and working closely with financial and legal professionals, potential buyers can gain a comprehensive understanding of the business's financial health, growth potential, and any potential risks or challenges. This information is vital in making an informed decision and maximizing the chances of a successful acquisition.

Getting the Real Facts

If properly investigated, you will find out that a business which is for sale has not been doing well, and might be relatively cheaper to buy that business. The incoming owner(s) must make sure, that they are capable of transforming an unprofitable business to a successful business.

There could be hidden reasons why the person selling the business want to sell the business, but does not want to share with the incoming owner(s). For example, a new megastore has recently opened in the same location or competitors are moving into the area or that a nearby factory has closed causing customers to leave the area. If you are considering buying or taking over an established business, you must find out as much as possible about the location in which the business is located, and about any future events which might harm the business, even if you are familiar with the area.

The Asking Price of the Business

The asking price of a business refers to the amount of money that the owner is seeking in exchange for selling their business. It is the initial price set by the seller, and it serves as a starting point for negotiations between the seller and potential buyers.

Determining the asking price for a business can be a complex process that takes into account a variety of factors. These factors may include the financial performance of the business, its assets and liabilities, market conditions, industry trends, and the overall value of similar businesses in the market.

To arrive at a reasonable asking price, business owners may enlist the help of professional business valuators or appraisers who can conduct a thorough analysis of the business and provide an objective assessment of its worth. This assessment may involve reviewing financial statements, assessing the business's market position and potential, and considering any unique or valuable assets or intellectual property that the business possesses.

It is important for business owners to set a realistic asking price that accurately reflects the value of their business. Setting the price too high may deter potential buyers and prolong the selling process, while setting it too low may result in the owner not receiving fair compensation for their hard work and investment.

In summary, the asking price of a business is the initial amount set by the owner when selling their business. It is determined through a careful assessment of the business's financial performance, market conditions, and other relevant factors. Setting a reasonable asking price is crucial for attracting potential buyers and ensuring a fair transaction for both parties involved.

The Make Up of the Value of a Business
The overall value of a business is made up of two main features:-

- The accepted total value of its **"assets"** – meaning what it actually owns, **less** the total value of its **"liabilities"** – meaning what it owes, to others.

- Ability of the business to generate profits for the owner(s), and to keep on earning profits.

Values of Assets and Liabilities

The value of assets and liabilities is an essential aspect of accounting and financial analysis. Assets refer to the resources owned by a company or individual that have economic value and can be converted into cash. Examples of assets include cash, accounts receivable, inventory, and property.

Determining the value of assets and liabilities is crucial for financial reporting and decision-making. It helps assess the financial health of an entity and provides insight into its ability to meet its obligations. This information is also necessary for calculating key financial ratios, such as the debt-to-equity ratio, which provides an indication of a company's financial leverage.

In order to determine the value of assets and liabilities, various methods can be used. Assets can be valued at historical cost, fair value, or net realizable value, depending on the accounting standards being followed. Liabilities are typically recorded at their face value or the amount required to settle the obligation. The exact value of stocks of good or materials should be worked out on the date of sale, not before, after a careful stock count. A valuation based on the cost prices of different stock items can then be made. Any item which are out of date have little or no value, and so should not be included the count.

Ultimately, the value of assets and liabilities serves as a foundation for understanding the financial position of a business or individual. It provides a snapshot of their financial resources and obligations, helping stakeholders make informed decisions based on accurate and reliable financial information. Assets and liabilities are key components of a company's financial statements and play a crucial role in determining a company's value.

Assets refer to the economic resources owned or controlled by a company that provide future benefits. These can include physical assets such as buildings, equipment, and inventory, as well as intangible assets like patents, trademarks, and goodwill. The value of assets is typically measured at their historical cost, less any depreciation or impairment.

Liabilities, on the other hand, are the obligations or debts that a company owes to external parties. These can include loans, accounts payable, accrued expenses, and other financial obligations. Like assets, liabilities are recorded at their historical cost, which is the amount owed at the time of acquisition.

Special Attributes

When considering the purchase of a business, it is essential to understand the special attributes that can greatly impact its value and potential for success. These special attributes refer to distinctive characteristics or features that set the business apart from others in the market. Identifying and analyzing these attributes is crucial for potential buyers in order to make informed decisions and assess the true value of the business.

One key special attribute to consider is the business's reputation and brand recognition. A well-established and respected brand can provide a significant competitive advantage, as it attracts a loyal customer base and enhances the business's overall market position. It is important to evaluate the strength of the brand and assess how it aligns with the target market and industry trends. These are some examples of special features a business might have which can help it do better than similar businesses:-

- A business might own "patents" (the right to use) a particular invention.

- A business might own the "copyright" (the right to reproduce) particular publications, musical works, films or video, etc.

- A business might have a franchise for the area.

- A business might have agreements or contract with government agencies or big clients.

- A business might be the sole agent or sole distributor for particular products. These terms mean that the business is the only authorized seller or provider.

- A business might be situated in a particularly good position; for example, a take-away restaurant near a college.

Another special attribute to look for is the uniqueness of the products or services offered by the business. Differentiation is key in today's competitive market, and businesses that offer innovative or niche products often have a higher value proposition. Understanding the intellectual property, patents, or proprietary technology associated with the business can provide insights into its potential for growth and future profitability.

Additionally, the business's customer base and strong relationships with key clients or suppliers can be a significant special attribute. A diversified and loyal customer base reduces the risk of revenue concentration and provides stability. Evaluating the quality of customer relationships, their purchasing patterns, and the potential for cross-selling or up-selling opportunities is crucial.

Financial performance is another important special attribute to consider. Analyzing historical financial statements, profitability ratios, and cash flow patterns provides insights into the business's financial health and potential for future growth. Buyers should also assess any relevant industry trends and market dynamics that may impact the business's financial performance.

Finally, the qualifications and skills of the existing management team can be a critical special attribute. A competent and experienced management team can drive the business's success and ensure a smooth transition for new owners. Buyers should evaluate the depth of management talent and assess the potential for employee retention and development.

In conclusion, understanding and evaluating special attributes are essential when assessing the value and potential of a business for sale. These attributes, including reputation, product uniqueness, customer base, financial performance, and management talent, can greatly impact the business's success and profitability. Conducting comprehensive due diligence and seeking professional advice can help buyers make informed decisions and maximize their chances of acquiring a successful and thriving business.

Goodwill

Goodwill in business refers to the intangible value of a business that is based on its reputation, customer relations, brand recognition, and other non-physical assets. It is an important concept in accounting and is considered an intangible asset on a company's balance sheet. Goodwill can be built over time through the consistent delivery of high-quality products or services, strong customer relationships, effective marketing and branding strategies, and a positive reputation in the industry. It represents the added value that a company has beyond its tangible assets, such as buildings, equipment, and inventory.

Goodwill plays a crucial role in determining the overall value of a business, as it can contribute significantly to its marketability and future profitability. When a business is sold, goodwill is typically factored into the purchase price. It can also be impaired if there are changes in market conditions, customer perception, or other factors that affect the company's reputation and future earnings potential.

From a financial standpoint, the value of goodwill is not easily quantifiable, as it is subjective and dependent on various factors. However, companies are required to periodically assess the value of their goodwill and test it for impairment if necessary. The impairment test involves comparing the carrying value of goodwill to its fair value, and if the carrying value exceeds the fair value, an impairment loss must be recognized.

In summary, goodwill represents the intangible value of a business that is based on its reputation, customer relations, brand recognition, and other non-physical assets. It contributes to the overall value of a company and is an important consideration in financial reporting and business valuations.

How the price is to be paid

This will depend on what price you would be ready to pay to purchase a business. The seller might accept payment in full or by installments over a number of months or years. In this case, a legal agreement would have to be drafted, signed and dated by all the parties involved.

Assistance Offered

The out-going owner(s) of a business might offer assistance to you, as the new owner of the business if you lack experience of running the business. The vendor has been assured of monthly income for an agreed period of time he or she is willingly to assist.

Avoiding Competition

This is a very serious matter that should not be overlooked. There is a possibility that after purchasing or taking over an established business from the previous owner(s), he or she (they) might start another similar business that you bought from him or her (they) in the same area. In this case, a legal agreement should entered by both parties stating that former owner will not start a competitive business in the same area for a stipulated number of years after the sale of the business.

The Sale Agreement

A sales agreement is an essential document used in business transactions to outline the terms and conditions of a sale. It is a legally binding agreement between a buyer and a seller that sets forth the rights and obligations of each party involved in the transaction. This agreement serves to protect the interests of both parties and ensures that the transaction is carried out smoothly and in accordance with the agreed-upon terms.

The sales agreement typically includes important details such as the names and addresses of the buyer and seller, a detailed description of the product or service being sold, the purchase price, payment terms, delivery terms, warranties, and any other relevant terms and conditions. It may also include provisions for dispute resolution, indemnification, and limitations of liability. By having a well-drafted sales agreement in place, businesses can minimize the potential for misunderstandings, disputes, and legal issues that may arise during the course of a sale. It provides a clear framework for the sales transaction and ensures that both parties are aware of their rights and obligations.

It is crucial for businesses to consult legal professionals or experienced attorneys when drafting a sales agreement to ensure that all necessary provisions are included and that it complies with applicable laws and regulations. This will help protect the interests of the business and provide a solid foundation for successful business transactions.If the business you are buying is a limited liability company (LLC), you will be buying share in it. The number of shares you are buying must be transferred into your name from the names of the present owner(s) of the shares.

Buying Into a Partnership

The opportunity to buy into a partnership is sometimes offered to someone who is hard working and already working as an employee for the partnership firm, or offered to outsiders to join a partnership. Buying into an existing partnership business can be done in two ways: - *Buying out an existing partner and Buying into an expanded partnership.*

Buying out an Existing Partner

When existing partner in a partnership business wish to sell the part of the partnership firm he or she owns, and leave, the remaining partners may have to agree to your purchase of part of the business. In this case, there should be a legal sales agreement between you and the partner whom you are buying out of the partnership firm.

Buying into an Expanded Partnership

This refers to existing partners considering adding new partner (s) one or more than one to the partnership. There are reasons partnership firms add new partners, and that might be because, the firm is expanding or performing well and the need to spread duties and responsibilities or the business need specialist skills or knowledge or the business need more capital to expand, and so on. Before joining a partnership firm, you need to know why you might be accepted and the benefits after paying. In this instance, you should enter a new **partnership agreement** with the remaining partner(s).

The Business Premises

The property (land/or building) from which the business operates might attract the attention of an attorney (a lawyer). The services of an attorney (a lawyer) most not be ignored when purchasing a business premises to avoid costly and damaging mistakes to businesses operating from the premises.

Included in the Purchase Price

In some cases, the property where a business operates might be personal property (land and/or building) of the seller (s), and the purchase price of the business might not include the property (land and/or building). But if the purchase price of the business includes the property (land and/or building), an attorney (a lawyer) will help arrange the transfer of ownership of the property (land and/or building) to the new buyer(s).

In a situation, where the business being bought is a limited liability company, the ownership of the company will transfer the shares to the new buyer(s). But the ownership of the property (land and/or building) will still be owned by the company and will not be transferred to the new buyer(s).

Rented or Leased Premises

A business pay rent to owner(s) of the rental property for the right to use the premises. The owner(s) of the property is called the **landlord**. The person(s) or business renting the premises is called the **tenant**. Sometimes the property is managed by an agent of the landlord.

The Lease

A written lease agreement is recommended if your intention is to rent premises of a new or an existing business. The lease agreement will set out conditions under which the premises will be rented or leased. The lease agreement must be signed by the landlord or agent of the landlord and the tenant(s). It is advisable not to sign a lease agreement offered by a landlord or agent until you have carefully read it and agreed to terms of it, or you have had it looked at by an attorney (a lawyer).

It not advisable to operate a business from rented premises without a proper, legal lease. Premises offered for rent on a monthly basis can be legally terminated by a landlord. The landlord can give a tenant one month notice or less to vacate, the premises. If this happened, and you could not quickly find suitable alternative premises, your business could be harmed.

Matters to Look at in Leases

When entering into a lease agreement, there are several important factors to consider and thoroughly examine before making any commitments. These matters are critical to ensure that both parties are protected and well-informed throughout the duration of the lease. *You should pay special attention on the following points in a lease agreement.*

The first aspect to address is the **lease term**. It is essential to clearly define the length of the lease, including any renewal options, termination clauses, and provisions for lease extensions. Additionally, both parties should agree on the start and end dates of the lease and any associated timelines for notice periods or rent adjustments.

Next, parties must carefully review the **rental payment terms**. This includes determining the frequency of rental payments, the amount due, and any specific methods of payment that are accepted. It is also crucial to understand if there are any penalties or late fees for missed or delayed payments and to clarify how payment discrepancies will be resolved.

Another critical consideration is the **condition of the leased property**. Before signing the lease, a comprehensive inspection should be conducted to document the current state of the property. This will help avoid any disputes regarding pre-existing damages or issues. Additionally, both parties should clearly outline their responsibilities for repairs, maintenance, and any potential remodeling or renovations that may be required throughout the lease term.

Furthermore, it is crucial to thoroughly understand the **rights and obligations** of each party. This includes determining who is responsible for utilities, property taxes, insurance, and other associated costs. It is also important to address any **restrictions or limitations** on the use of the leased property, such as zoning regulations or noise restrictions, and to outline the consequences of non-compliance.

Finally, the lease should include **provisions for dispute resolution** and an exit strategy. Parties should agree on the procedures for resolving any conflicts that may arise during the lease term, such as mediation or arbitration. It is also essential to outline the process for terminating the lease, including notice requirements and any penalties or fees associated with early termination.

Overall, the matters to look at in leases encompass a wide range of factors that require careful consideration and negotiation. Both parties should seek professional legal advice to ensure that their rights and interests are adequately protected throughout the lease agreement.

When it comes to looking for leases, it's important to carefully consider the area in which the lease is located. The location of your business can have a significant impact on its success, so it's crucial to thoroughly research and analyze the area before committing to a lease agreement.

Area

When it comes to looking for leases, it's important to carefully consider the area in which the lease is located. The location of your business can have a significant impact on its success, so it's crucial to thoroughly research and analyze the area before committing to a lease agreement.

One of the first things you'll want to assess is the **demographics of the area**. You'll want to know the average age, income levels, and population density of the surrounding community. This information will give you a good understanding of your potential customer base and whether or not your target market aligns with the demographics of the area.

Another important factor to consider is the **competition in the area**. Are there already several businesses similar to yours in the vicinity? If so, how well are they doing? Can your business differentiate itself and attract customers despite the competition? Understanding the competitive landscape will help you determine if the area is a suitable location for your business.

Additionally, you'll want to **evaluate the accessibility and visibility** of the location. Is it easily accessible by major roads or public transportation? Is there ample parking for both employees and customers? Is the location visible to passing traffic? These factors can greatly impact the foot traffic and visibility your business receives, ultimately affecting its success.

Other important aspects to consider include the **safety of the area**, proximity to suppliers and vendors, zoning regulations and restrictions, and any potential future developments or changes that may impact the area.

By thoroughly examining these factors, you can make an informed decision about whether a specific lease in a certain area is the right move for your business. It's always a good idea to consult with a real estate professional who specializes in commercial leases to ensure you're making the best decision for your business's future success.

Property Space

When entering into a lease agreement, it is important to have a clear understanding of the amount of space you are renting. This can be determined by calculating the property space in either square meters or yards. To check the property space in square meters, you will need to measure the length and width of each room or area in the property. Multiply these two measurements together to get the square meterage of each individual space. Then, simply add up the square meterage of all the spaces to determine the total property space.

If you prefer to work with yards instead of square meters, the process is similar. Measure the length and width of each room or area in the property, and multiply these two measurements together to obtain the square yards of each individual space. Once you have the square yardage of each area, add them together to determine the total property space.

Checking the property space in either square meters or yards is crucial for ensuring that you are getting the amount of space you expect in your lease agreement. It also allows you to accurately compare different properties and make informed decisions about which one best suits your needs.

Rent or Rental

Parties must carefully review the rental payment terms. This includes determining the frequency of rental payments, the amount due, and any specific methods of payment that are accepted. It is also crucial to understand if there are any penalties or late fees for missed or delayed payments and to clarify how payment discrepancies will be resolved. Check how much is the rental and how it has to be paid. In some cases, rental has to be paid in advance, and on weekly, monthly and quarterly basis or at lengthy interval.

Dates

When entering into a lease agreement, it is crucial to carefully review and check the start dates and end dates specified in the agreement. This is an important step to ensure that both parties are clear on the duration of the lease and avoid any potential disputes or misunderstandings in the future.

Start dates and end dates in a lease agreement typically refer to the specific dates on which the tenant is granted access to the leased property and when the lease agreement will terminate. These dates are crucial as they establish the duration of the lease and outline the rights and obligations of both the landlord and the tenant.

When reviewing the start and end dates, it is important to ensure that they accurately reflect the agreed-upon period of occupancy. This can be done by cross-referencing the dates with any other relevant documents, such as emails or correspondence between the parties. It is also advisable to consult with legal counsel or a real estate professional to ensure that the dates align with local laws and regulations.

In addition, it is important to pay attention to any provisions in the lease agreement that may affect the start or end dates. For example, if there are any conditions or requirements that need to be fulfilled before the tenant can take possession of the property, such as repairs or renovations, these should be clearly stated in the agreement and accounted for in the start date.

Similarly, if there are any provisions that allow for an extension or renewal of the lease agreement, the terms and conditions should be clearly outlined to avoid any confusion or disputes when it comes to the end date.

By carefully reviewing and verifying the start and end dates in a lease agreement, both landlords and tenants can ensure clarity and avoid any potential complications or disagreements. It is always recommended to seek professional advice and thoroughly understand the terms of the lease agreement before signing to protect the rights and interests of all parties involved.

Renewal

One important aspect of being a landlord or property manager is ensuring that you are well-informed about the rights and responsibilities of both tenants and landlords. When it comes to lease agreements, it is essential to understand whether a tenant has the right to renew their lease for additional period on its expiry, and, if so, for what period and on what conditions.

In many jurisdictions, tenants are granted the right to renew their lease agreement. This means that as a landlord, you cannot terminate the tenancy at the end of the lease term if the tenant wishes to renew and complies with the necessary conditions.

To determine whether a tenant has the right to renew their lease agreement, you should start by reviewing the initial lease agreement. This document should outline the specific terms and conditions regarding lease renewal, including any requirements or limitations.

Next, check your local laws and regulations. Landlord-tenant laws vary from one jurisdiction to another and may offer additional protections or requirements for lease renewals. Familiarize yourself with these laws to ensure compliance and to understand the specific rights granted to tenants.

If you discover that a tenant does have the right to renew their lease, it is crucial to communicate with the tenant in a timely manner. Ideally, you should provide the tenant with a notice of the upcoming lease expiration at least 30 to 60 days in advance. This allows both parties to discuss their intentions and negotiate any changes or modifications to the lease agreement.

Remember, proper documentation is essential throughout the lease renewal process. Be sure to document all communications and agreements with the tenant, including any changes to the lease terms. This helps protect both parties and provides a clear record of the renewal process.

In summary, when it comes to determining whether a tenant has the right to renew their lease agreement, it is crucial to review the initial lease agreement, consult local laws and regulations, and communicate effectively with the tenant. By staying informed and following the necessary steps, you can ensure a smooth and compliant lease renewal process.

Change of Tenant

As per the lease agreement signed between the landlord and the tenant, any change in the tenancy requires the explicit consent of the landlord. This includes a change of tenant, whereby the current tenant wishes to transfer their rights and responsibilities to a new person or entity.

To initiate the process of changing a tenant, the current tenant must first submit a formal request to the landlord. This request should include the contact information and identification details of the proposed new tenant, as well as any relevant documents such as credit reports or references.

Upon receipt of the request, the landlord will review the proposed new tenant and assess their suitability based on their ability to meet the financial obligations outlined in the lease agreement, as well as their rental and credit history.

If the landlord approves the change of tenant, both the current tenant and the proposed new tenant will be required to sign 'consent' to change of tenant form. This form outlines the terms of the change and confirms that both parties agree to the transfer of rights and responsibilities.

It is important to note that the change of tenant does not release the current tenant from their obligations under the lease agreement. The new tenant will assume all of the rights and responsibilities outlined in the original lease, including the payment of rent and maintenance of the property.

A fee may be applicable for processing the change of tenant, and both parties should consult the lease agreement or seek legal advice for further information.

It is crucial for all parties involved to ensure that the change of tenant is done in accordance with the lease agreement and any applicable laws and regulations. Failure to obtain the landlord's consent or properly execute the change of tenant may result in legal consequences or breach of the lease agreement.

We recommend seeking professional legal advice when initiating a change of tenant in a lease agreement to ensure compliance with all requirements and protect the interests of both the landlord and the tenants involved.

Rent Reviews or Revisions

Rent reviews or revisions in a lease agreement are important considerations for both landlords and tenants. These mechanisms allow for adjustments to the rental amount over the course of the lease term, ensuring that the rent remains fair and reflective of market conditions.

Rent reviews can take different forms depending on the agreed terms between parties. The most common types include *fixed rent reviews*, *market rent reviews, and indexed rent reviews*.

Fixed rent reviews, involve predetermined increases in the rental amount at set intervals. This approach provides stability and predictability for both the landlord and tenant. However, it is essential to ensure that the fixed rent increase aligns with the current market conditions to avoid potential disputes.

Market rent reviews, on the other hand, determine the rental amount based on the prevailing market rates at the time of the review. This approach ensures that the rent remains competitive and reflects the value of the property within the current rental market. Professional property valuations and market research can be essential in determining the fair market rent.

Indexed rent reviews provide a mechanism for rent adjustments based on an agreed upon index, such as the Consumer Price Index (CPI). This approach takes into account inflation and provides a fair and objective way to adjust the rent over time. It is important to specify the index used and the frequency of review in the lease agreement.

Whether you are a landlord or a tenant, it is crucial to carefully review and negotiate the rent review provisions in the lease agreement. Consideration should be given to factors such as the frequency of reviews, the method of review, and any applicable caps or limitations. Seeking legal advice from a qualified professional can help ensure that the rent review provisions align with your objectives and comply with legal requirements.

Other Payments Over and Above the Rent

When entering into a lease agreement, it is important to understand that there may be additional payments required beyond just the rent. These additional payments often referred to as **"other payment**s,"** can vary depending on the terms of the lease agreement and the specific property.

One common type of additional payment is the security deposit. This is a refundable amount of money that the tenant provides to the landlord at the beginning of the lease term. The purpose of the security deposit is to protect the landlord in case the tenant causes damage to the property or fails to fulfill their obligations under the lease agreement. The amount of the security deposit is typically determined based on the monthly rent amount, and it is held by the landlord until the end of the lease term.

In some cases, the lease agreement may include provisions for additional payments such as utility fees or common area maintenance fees. These fees are typically used to cover the cost of maintaining and operating shared spaces or utilities within a multi-unit property, such as a shopping center or office building. The amount and method of payment for these fees will be outlined in the lease agreement.

It is important to carefully review the lease agreement and understand all of the additional payments that may be required before signing the document.

If you have any questions or concerns about the specific terms of the lease agreement, it is recommended to consult with a legal professional or a leasing agent who can provide guidance and clarification.

Always make sure that:

1. Your lease is legal for any property rented by you or your business. and that

2. The period and conditions of the lease agreement are fair and reasonable.

Commercial Lease

Share Holdings and Share Transfers

The shares held by an individual or legal entity that is registered by a company as the legal owner of shares. The number of share held might increase or decrease from time to time. For example, Tim held 5,000 shares in a company, and later bought some of the unissued shares, or bought some or all of the shares held by another investor in the same company: Tim shareholding would increase. If at a later date Tim decided to sell some of his shares in the company, to one of the investors in the company, or to another party if any of the existing investors in company did not want to buy some or all of the shares; Tim shareholding would decrease. It is important to note that not only people may hold shares in a company; other entities might hold shares.

Practical Examples: E

Joseph converted his motor vehicle repair business into a limited liability company (LLC): *"Martyrs' Garage Ltd"* and wants to buy a motor spare parts business which is also a limited liability company called *"Mid Town Spares Ltd"*. Joseph could buy shares from the current shareholders of *"Mid Town Spares Ltd"*. **Or** Joseph could buy some shares in his own name, and *"Martyrs' Garage Ltd"* could buy some in **its** name as the company has the legal right to do.

A company called *"Smith and Sons Ltd"* might approach a bank or another financial institution to buy its unissued share capital. The bank or financial institution might agree to buy some or all of the unissued shares, and become a shareholder in *"Smith and Sons Ltd"*.

It is important to note that shares are not always sold for cash by an individual or entity in order to be transferred to another individual or entity. In some cases, an individual might inherit shares, for example from a deceased relative.

When share(s) are transferred to an individual or organization; a new share certificate or more than one must be issued in the name of the replacement shareholder(s). Old share certificate(s) returned to the company secretary for cancellation. According to governing law, written records of all shares issues, changes in ownership, etc., must be maintained.

Board of Directors

The board of directors is a governing body that oversees the activities of a company or organization. It is comprised of a group of individuals who are elected or appointed to represent the shareholders or stakeholders of the organization. The primary role of the board of directors is to make important decisions and provide guidance on strategic direction, financial matters, to turn the business *'on behalf of'* the shareholders in such a way that satisfactory profits are made by it, and overall management of the organization.

The specific responsibilities and duties of the board of directors can vary depending on the type of organization and its legal structure. However, some common functions of the board include setting corporate goals and objectives, hiring and evaluating senior executives, approving budgets and financial plans, and ensuring compliance with laws and regulations. The board is like the **"watchdog"** of the shareholders interest and investments. As the **"watchdog"** of the shareholders, it must protect the capital invested by the shareholders in the company.

Board members are typically individuals with diverse backgrounds and areas of expertise who bring valuable perspectives and experiences to the table. They may be former executives, industry experts, or individuals with specialized knowledge in areas such as finance, marketing, or legal affairs.

The board of directors operates in a fiduciary capacity, meaning they have a legal obligation to act in the best interests of the organization and its stakeholders. They are expected to exercise sound judgment, exercise due diligence, and act in an ethical and transparent manner.

Overall, the board of directors plays a crucial role in ensuring the long-term success and sustainability of the organization. By providing oversight, strategic guidance, and accountability, they help steer the organization towards its goals and objectives while safeguarding the interests of the shareholders or stakeholders.

Executive and Non-Executive Directors

Executive and non-executive directors are both important roles within a company's board of directors. They each have distinct responsibilities and play different roles in the decision-making and governance of the organization.

An executive director is typically a member of the company's management team and is involved in the day-to-day operations and strategic direction of the business. They are usually responsible for managing the company's operations, implementing the board's decisions, and ensuring the organization is meeting its financial and operational goals. Executive directors are often appointed based on their expertise and experience in a specific industry or function.

On the other hand, **a non-executive director** is an independent member of the board who is not involved in the daily management of the company. They bring an outside perspective and are responsible for providing objective and impartial advice to the executive team. **Non-executive directors** are often appointed for their industry knowledge, strategic thinking, and ability to provide oversight and accountability to the company's management team. They are also responsible for ensuring the company is adhering to legal and regulatory requirements, maintaining good corporate governance practices, and safeguarding the interests of shareholders.

The roles of executive and non-executive directors can vary depending on the size and nature of the company. In some cases, a director may serve in both capacities, while in others; there may be a clear separation between executive and non-executive roles. Regardless of the specific roles and responsibilities, both executive and non-executive directors have a fiduciary duty to act in the best interests of the company and its stakeholders.

In conclusion, executive directors are involved in the day-to-day management and operations of the company, while non-executive directors provide independent oversight and guidance. The combination of these roles helps to ensure effective governance, strategic decision-making, and the long-term success of the organization.

Company 'Officials'

Company Officer means any person who is approved by the Board of Directors of the Company to manage the business and operations of the Company. The Company Officer is often called the **'managing director'** (MD) or "chief executive" (CEO). The Company Officers meet from time to time to discuss matters concerning the company, how the Company is doing, the profit it is making and other matters relating to its operations. These **'board meetings'** is headed by the **'chairman'**. In small Company, the meeting is headed by the managing director who might also be the chairman. Any decisions made and agreed must be recorded in the 'minutes' of the board meetings and maintained.

Directors' Fees

This applies to payment for time spent by directors on attending board meetings. The payment may be called **'directors fee'**, and only payable to directors not involved in running the business. Director responsible for running the business will receive a salary or wage approved by the board, and might be paid a small director fee in addition to salary or wage. In some cases, all earnings of directors are called directors fees.

Dividends

Dividends are a form of payment that a company may distribute to its shareholders. These payments are typically made in cash, although they can also be in the form of additional shares of stock. Dividends are a way for a company to distribute its profits to its shareholders, who are the owners of the company.

Dividends are usually paid out on a regular basis, such as quarterly or annually, and the amount of the dividend is typically based on the company's profits. The board of directors of a company will determine the dividend amount and the frequency of the payments. They may also choose to adjust the dividend amount based on various factors, such as the company's financial performance or future plans.

Dividends are an important consideration for investors, as they provide a source of income in addition to any capital gains that may be realized from the increase in the value of the stock. Companies that pay regular dividends are often considered to be stable and well-established, which can make them attractive to investors looking for a steady income stream.

It is important to note that not all companies pay dividends. Some companies, particularly newer or growing companies, may choose to reinvest their profits back into the business rather than distribute them to shareholders. This is often the case with technology companies or startups, where there may be a greater need for capital to fund research and development or expansion efforts.

In conclusion, dividends are a form of payment that a company may distribute to its shareholders as a way to share its profits. They can provide investors with a steady income stream and are an important consideration when evaluating potential investments.

Statutory Obligations

Statutory obligations refer to legal requirements that individuals, organizations, or businesses must comply with. These obligations are set forth in statutes and legislation enacted by the government. They are binding and enforceable by law.

Statutory obligations can vary depending on the jurisdiction and industry. For example, businesses may have statutory obligations related to labor laws, taxes, health and safety regulations, environmental standards, and consumer protection. Individuals may have statutory obligations related to paying taxes, obeying traffic laws, and fulfilling jury duty, among others.

Compliance with statutory obligations is crucial to avoiding legal penalties and maintaining a good reputation. Failure to meet these obligations can result in fines, lawsuits, or even criminal prosecution. It is essential for individuals and businesses to stay informed about their statutory obligations and take the necessary steps to fulfill them.

To ensure compliance, organizations often have dedicated departments or personnel responsible for monitoring changes in legislation and ensuring that the company's operations align with the statutory requirements. This may involve implementing policies, conducting regular audits, and maintaining accurate records. For example, the board of directors must make sure the company applies for and obtain any **trade licenses** needed in the country for its business activities.

The board must ensure the company pays any **taxes** or **contributions** for which it is liable, and 'Annual Return' (or "report" in some countries) must be submitted to *"Registrar of Companies"* once each year. The **'Annual Return'** must indicate the number shares the company has issued and their value, the names and addresses of its shareholders and directors. The 'Annual Return' must also state whether there have been changes since the previous annual return or "report".

Additionally, it is advisable to seek legal counsel or consult with experts in specific fields to ensure a thorough understanding of statutory obligations. Lawyers, accountants, and industry-specific professionals can provide valuable guidance and assistance in navigating the complex landscape of statutory obligations.

In summary, statutory obligations are legal requirements that individuals and businesses must comply with to avoid legal consequences. Understanding and fulfilling these obligations are vital for maintaining legal compliance and upholding ethical standards.

CHAPTER QUESTIONS FOUR – CHAPTER 4

Recommended Answers to the Questions-against which you may compare your answers-are in the Appendix after the end of this Chapter. The maximum mark which may be awarded for each Question appears in brackets at the end of the Question.

No.1. Describe circumstances in which you might consider buying a business as a "going" concern rather than starting a new one. (maximum 40 marks)

No.2. (a) Say you were considering buying a business as a "going concern". Why would you need to find out exactly why it was being offered for sale? (maximum 20 marks)

(b) To what matters would you pay special attention before signing the lease for premises you might rent for a business? (maximum 20 marks)

No.3. Place a tick in the box against the **one correct** statement in each set.
(a) In business the term "creditor" means:
1.☐ a customer who has bought goods without paying for them at once.
2.☐ a person or organization to whom money is owed.
3.☐ a customer who is satisfied with products bought and recommends the business to others.
4.☐ a person who agrees to be responsible for a loan made by a bank.

(b) With regard to premises, "rent" refers to:
1.☐ the owner of the building from whom they leased.
2.☐ the document which sets out the conditions under which the premises are leased.
3.☐ a tear in floor coverings or curtains.
4.☐ the sum paid to the landlord for the right to use the premises.

(c) Dividends are:
1.☐ payments made to shareholders being a proportion of the profits made by a company.
2.☐ sections of its premises divided from each other by partitions.
3.☐ people or organizations who owe money to a business.
4.☐ the various "parts" of a firm owned by each of its partners.

(d) A "going concern" is:
1.☐ a business involved in transportation, by road, sea, air or water.
2.☐ an established and functioning business.
3.☐ a customer leaving the premises of a business without buying.
4.☐ a business moving to new premises.

(e) Executive directors:
1.☐ work full time for the company.
2.☐ are similar to sleeping partners and do not work in the business.
3.☐ are the most senior directors of the company.
4.☐ are the only ones allowed to attend board meetings.

No.4. Place a tick in the box against the one correct statement in each set.

(a) *If a profitable business is bought, it is important that*:
1.☐ the agreed purchase price is paid in full at once.
2.☐ a legally binding sale agreement is signed by all parties involved.
3.☐ the premises remain the property of the business.
4.☐ the new owner runs the business in exactly the same way as before.

(b) *A business gains "goodwill" which arises because*:
1.☐ the hard work of its owners secures and keeps satisfied customers.
2.☐ a partner dies and leaves money to the business.
3.☐ it needs them to resell to its customers.
4.☐ it allows it to use the premises from which it operates.

(c) The board of directors may be called the shareholders' "watchdog":
1.☐ because it does what they tell it as any other pet would do.
2.☐ because it earns the largest share of profits made by the company.
3.☐ because its duty is to protect their interests and investments.
4.☐ because it checks that all doors and windows are securely locked.

(d) A "lease":
1.☐ arises when the expenses of a business are greater than its income.
2.☐ is the lowest price for which a product may be sold.
3.☐ is a debt which a business owes to a person or organization.
4.☐ sets out the conditions under which premises will be rented.

(e) Debtors of a business are:
1.☐ people or business to which it owes debts.
2.☐ records of the values of income, expenditure, assets and liabilities.
3.☐ people or organizations who owe debts to it.
4.☐ the values of its assets after wear and tear.

(2 marks for a statement correctly ticked – maximum 20

Chapter 5
FURNISHING AND EQUIPPING
THE BUSINESS PREMISES

Factors which dictate needs of the businesses:

The type of business being conducted, the size of the premises, the number of employees, the type of customers, and the budget allocated for the furnishing and equipping of the business premises are some of the factors that dictate the needs of the business. It is important for the business owner to carefully consider these factors in order to create a comfortable and functional work environment that can help improve productivity and customer satisfaction.

The furnishing – the furniture, fittings and fixtures – and the equipment needed will depend on various factors, such as the purpose of the space, the budget allocated, and the design preferences of the owner.

- ✓ The type of business, its size, and its activities will determine the necessary furnishing, including furniture, fittings, and fixtures, as well as equipment. For instance, a retail store would require a different setup of furnishings and equipment compared to a workshop or a business that provides services and needs office space.

- ✓ When furnishing and equipping business premises, several factors need to be considered. One of the most important factors is the shape and size of the premises and how different sections will be used. For instance, in a retail business, the area designated for customers (the "selling area") needs to be attractively decorated, with suitable floor covering, to make it more appealing to customers. On the other hand, when it comes to the stockroom, it is necessary to have easily cleanable painted walls and a durable and easy-to-clean floor covering.

- ✓ The number of visitors to a business premises can vary greatly depending on the nature of the business. Some businesses may receive a large number of visitors on a daily basis, while others may have very few. It's important to take into consideration what customers or clients are comfortable with in terms of the number of visitors and their expectations. It's true that customers of some businesses have higher expectations when it comes to the quality of furnishings compared to customers of other businesses. It largely depends on the type of business and the target audience it caters to.

✓ As a business owner, it's important to consider what you can afford before making any purchases. You don't always have to buy brand new furniture or equipment, especially if it's for areas of the premises that won't be seen by customers. There are often great deals to be found at auction sales or through for sale advertisements in newspapers for pre-owned furniture and equipment that can still be put to good use.

When starting a new business in rented premises, it's common for the space to be empty or nearly empty. Even if the previous tenant was running a business, the walls and ceilings might already be painted and some floor covering or carpeting might have been laid. However, it's possible that none of these are suitable for your new business due to age, dirt or fading. Assuming you need to start from scratch, let's take a look at what needs to be done to get the premises ready for business.

Layout of the business premises

The layout of a business premises plays a crucial role in creating a conducive environment for employees to work efficiently. It involves the arrangement of physical spaces, such as offices, workstations, meeting rooms, and common areas, to optimize workflow and productivity. A well-planned layout can also enhance the overall look and feel of the workplace, making it more appealing to clients and visitors.

It's important for any business, whether it's a shop, office, workshop, factory, or eating place, to have an efficient layout of its premises. This requires careful planning and a rough sketch, drawn to scale, can be very helpful. The total area and sections of the premises can be allocated to various activities, such as selling, office, stockroom, and so on.

Sometimes, alterations are needed so that the premises can be used for its intended purpose(s). Partition walls may need to be erected to separate different sections from one another. For example, a stockroom for materials and components should be separated from a finished goods stockroom and both should be separated from the production area, offices, and so on. This ensures maximum efficiency and productivity.

The Multi-Room Layout

The Multi-Room Layout is a common form of office layout that comprises two or more rooms, which may be situated on different floors or buildings. Such a layout is common in enterprises that have grown over a period of time, and the demands on the office have necessitated the allocation of more space wherever it has been available. On the other hand, it may also be brought about by the decentralization of functions, such as clerical work.

One of the disadvantages of this type of layout is that employees waste a considerable amount of time moving around the building(s) collecting and delivering information, records, and other documents, even with the use of an internal communication system. However, one advantage of this layout is that it provides a certain amount of privacy, while reducing the number of distractions.

The Open-Plan Layout

The open-plan layout refers to a large room where a number of employees work together, usually performing similar tasks. The room may be divided into sections by partitions, which could be made of glass and no higher than a meter. This style of layout offers the advantage of easy access to information, records, and documents, without having to move far. It also requires fewer machines and equipment of each type compared to the multi-room layout.

Movable partitions add flexibility to the open-plan layout and make rearrangement possible if the need arises. For instance, the workload of some sections may decrease while others increase at certain times of the year.

Supervision of employees working in an open-plan room is often easier, and it may require fewer supervisors. It is also easier to rearrange workloads in case of absences due to holidays or illnesses, or during busy times. A manager or supervisor may have a private office at one end of the main room, with glass panels in the walls to observe the main room and exercise control, while still providing some privacy.

Once the activities in each section have been determined, furniture and equipment can be arranged accordingly. The ideal layout for a business may not be possible due to the shape or size of the premises. However, the final layout should prioritize convenience, comfort, and safety for both customers and employees.

Regulations

It is important for shops, offices, factories, and other business premises to comply with safety regulations to ensure the well-being of their employees and visitors. The regulations cover various aspects such as sanitation facilities, safety measures, and a healthy environment. Before any modifications are made to the premises, it is essential to ensure that they comply with the regulations. Any necessary alterations should be made to meet the standards and provide a safe and healthy environment for everyone.

Electrical Fittings

Many business premises, particularly in older buildings, lack sufficient electrical plug sockets for the numerous machines used in modern businesses. Additionally, there may not be enough electrical light fixtures on walls or ceilings. The issue of electrical wiring should be addressed before any redecoration is carried out, before new floor covering is installed, and before furniture and machines are moved into the premises. The assistance of an electrician will be required. Some machines, particularly those in a workshop or factory, may require heavy-duty cabling and sockets.

Good lighting is essential in most business premises. Customers must be able to see clearly in order to work efficiently. In stockrooms, good lighting is required to enable the rapid location of goods and materials when needed. People working in workshops and factories require good lighting to avoid mistakes and accidents.

You may indicate on your plan where additional plug sockets and light fixtures will be required. This will be determined by the location of the machines, customers, and workers. Your plan will also serve as a guide for the electrician.

Telephones

In today's business world, a telephone or fax machine is a must-have. Usually, a telephone line will already be installed in your business premises, but it might have been disconnected. If that's the case, you will need to contact your local telephone provider to have the line transferred to your name or your business name and reconnected. Alternatively, you can request a new line installation.

Many businesses require several extensions and multiple incoming telephone lines. It's best to contact your local telephone provider to check if they can provide the required number of lines. Sometimes, an automatic switchboard, known as a PABX, is also needed. It's essential to mark on your plan where additional telephone sockets are needed, depending on where people needing to use a telephone will work.

Installation procedures may vary from country to country. In some countries, only employees of the telephone provider can do the installation, while in others, an electrician can fit the telephone cabling and sockets, possibly doing the electric wiring at the same time. It's always best to have the telephone installation done before any redecoration, before laying any new floor covering, and before furniture and machines are in place.

Computers

We will discuss computers in more detail later, but for now, let's focus on where they should be placed in the building. If there is only one computer, it should be located near an electrical socket. However, if there are multiple units that will be connected to a network, additional computer sockets and electrical sockets will be necessary. Your plan should include the locations for the computers, which will serve as a guide for the electrician and anyone else responsible for installing the cabling.

Walls and Ceilings

It is important to always keep these areas clean. They may require painting before moving in and at regular intervals after. Typically, white, off-white, or cream paint colors are used as they provide a bright and cheerful feel. However, other colors may be used to match the business type. For instance, yellow, orange, red, and brown can create a warm and exciting atmosphere in stores selling clothes for teenagers. On the other hand, green and blue tend to create a cool feeling, which can be ideal for an ice-cream parlor, café, or restaurant.

Floor Coverings

When selecting floor coverings, it is important to consider the climate of the country. In cooler areas, carpeting may be necessary to provide warmth. In warmer countries, cooler materials may be needed. The floor coverings chosen should be durable as they will experience a lot of foot traffic. Ideally, they should also match or complement the colors of the walls and ceilings. It is recommended to wait until any electrical, carpentry, or cabling work has been completed before laying new floor coverings. Additionally, it is best to wait until after painting the walls and ceilings as well.

Heating and/or Cooling

Heating and cooling are essential for ensuring the comfort of customers and employees, depending on the climate of a country. Fans or heaters can be used, as appropriate, to provide the required temperature. Although air-conditioning units are expensive, they might be the most suitable option for some premises.

Furniture

The type of furniture needed for a business depends on the activities and areas within the premises. For instance, a retail shop will require counters, display cabinets, shelves or racks for their selling areas, while the office area will need desks, chairs, filing cabinets, and more. The stock room will need storage shelves or racks and lockable cabinets for small and valuable items.

In some showrooms, desks and chairs are used to attend to customers while they are seated instead of standing at a counter. Counter units may have solid or glass tops, which are suitable for displaying goods. Some readymade counter units are available, while others may need to be customized to fit the size, shape, and layout of the premises.

A desk-like unit with a flat working surface, drawers, shelves, and pigeon holes can be fitted to the rear of a counter to allow the staff to work comfortably while not actually attending to customers. This also helps keep the counter tops clear and tidy.

The appearance and decor of the selling area of a business should be attractive and inviting. This is because prospective customers must be persuaded to enter the premises and once inside, to stay inside and make a purchase. The premises should be comfortable, visually pleasing, and especially if customers have to wait to be attended. It is important to note that all furniture items are assets of the business and have monetary value. If any furniture is lost, damaged, or destroyed, the business will lose its value, and money will have to be spent to replace them. Hence, it is necessary to protect and insure them.

Machinery and Equipment

The type, size, and number of machines and equipment required for a business depend on its type and size. For instance, a shop or store may only need cash registers and a computer, while an office or service business may require a computer, fax machine, photocopier, and other similar equipment. On the other hand, a factory or workshop will need different machinery depending on the products they manufacture, repair or service.

Some businesses may require complex and expensive machinery, which they may not be able to afford to pay for in full or cash. In such cases, there are two financing options worth considering. These options may be available in your country, and they include: - *- Financing the machinery and equipment through leasing agreements.- Financing the machinery and equipment through Hire Purchase (HP) or installment payments.*

Hiring, Renting or Leasing

When a business needs a piece of machinery, equipment or furniture, they can make an agreement with a financial institution, like a bank, to hire, rent, or lease the item. The value of the item is determined beforehand, and the business makes regular payments that include interest. Although the business gets to use the item(s), they don't own it, so it's not considered an asset. In some countries, tax allowances are permitted on hire, rental, and leasing payments. It's recommended to consult with an accountant or tax specialist in your country to better understand the tax implications.

Hire Purchase (Installment Payment)

When a customer pays a deposit for an item, they are only allowed to use it but do not become the legal owner immediately. The customer should sign an agreement to pay the remaining balance, which is the price less the deposit paid, plus interest in regular installments. It is only after the customer pays all the installments that they become the owner of the item(s).

In some countries, paying the installments may attract tax concessions.

Regardless of whether machinery and equipment are owned by a business or not, they are assets that have monetary value. If any of them are lost, damaged, or destroyed, the business will experience a loss in their value and may even be unable to operate. The business will have to pay money to replace them. Therefore, they need to be regularly serviced, repaired, and maintained. They must also be protected from damage and theft, and insured.

Working Assets

As we learned in Chapter 1, the machines, equipment, and furniture owned by a business are considered as its **working assets**. These assets are acquired to enable the business to operate and perform its work. Unlike materials, they are not intended to be used up nor bought and sold like goods. Even if these assets are maintained regularly, they gradually lose value over time due to wear and tear, which is referred to as **depreciation**. We will look into this topic in more depth in Chapter 11.

Doors and Windows

Ensuring the safety of one's business is vital. To protect the materials, goods, tools, and machines from being stolen, it's essential to make sure that all doors and windows are secure and tight-fitting. Lockable doors and windows are necessary, and if needed, bars or shutters should be installed to protect the plate glass windows outside business hours. It's essential to close and lock any fanlights that let in fresh air at night and on weekends. It's crucial to keep the keys to the locks safe as the best locks are of no use if the keys are lost or compromised or if there are too many of them.

The Outside

To attract customers to your business premises, it is advisable to display at least one sign on the outside that states the name of your business and its activities. There are various types of signs available, ranging from large to small, painted on walls or boards affixed on the walls. Smaller signs may be metal, plastic, or wooden plaques placed near the entrance. The signs can also be banners, illuminated or even moving. Before affixing or erecting a sign, it is essential to check with the local council office if licenses or permits are required in your country.

Window Displays

In Chapter 3, we explained how many businesses rely on passing-trade. Displays in front or display windows can catch the attention of passers-by and create interest in products for sale. They can even create a desire to buy a product. Next time you walk through a busy shopping area, observe the reactions of people walking past showrooms or shops. You will see that they often stop to look into windows that have attractively displayed goods. This favorable attention is what businesses aim for. While looking at the display of goods, customers may get interested in a particular item and this may prompt them to enter the shop.

On the other hand, people tend to walk past windows where goods have been dumped carelessly, and if it's not possible to see any particular item clearly. Therefore, an attractive and eye-catching window display is the first step to attract favorable attention. A window display is primarily an appeal to the eyes, and an untidy, dirty or poorly designed window display will not attract favorable attention.

Designing and Creating Window Displays

While larger businesses may employ specialists called window dressers to design their windows and attract the attention of passers-by, most of the time it is the owner, manager, or staff of a business who design and create window displays. The main goal of designing a display is to ensure that it attracts favorable attention and that the products displayed are easily seen and identifiable.

To achieve this, the designer should first decide what features or factors would attract them in the proposed display. The display should then be planned on paper, including all the features considered important. Proper planning is essential, as a display that is not well-planned may not be as attractive as it could be. The plan can be modified until the display is deemed the best that can be built.

Once the plan is in place, the building of the display can begin. It is important to remember that the display is intended to appeal to the eyes of people outside the premises who will, it is hoped, stop and look into the window(s). Once the display has been completed, it should be viewed from the outside to determine the impact it will make on passers-by. If necessary, rearrangements or changes can be made to showcase the products to their best advantage.

The lighting in windows is crucial so that the displays in them can be seen clearly during the day and at night. Brightly lit, colorful window displays can be very attractive at night.

Services

Window displays are not just limited to physical items such as goods. They can also be utilized to showcase services for sale. For instance, tour operating stores can create attractive and eye-catching displays in their windows to draw attention towards their services.

To make the displays more appealing, you can incorporate bright and colorful posters, tour brochures, display cards, and cutouts. Additionally, models of aircrafts or ships can also be displayed to represent the services offered. For example, placing a pair of ski poles and ski boots against a white polystyrene background in a window can create a visual representation of a skiing holiday, enticing passers-by to enter the store and learn more about the available ski trips. This technique can be especially useful on hot days when people are looking for cooler holiday options.

Keeping Attraction

Business owners and managers must not become complacent about their displays, even if they are well-designed and effective. Over time, the display will become dusty, faded, and old-looking, and it will be less attractive to customers. Additionally, what may have caught people's attention the first or second time they saw it will not continue to do so. It is important to replace window displays frequently with new ones, featuring different products that appeal to different people. This will keep the display fresh, exciting, and attention-grabbing.

Some shops and stores have solid back windows which prevent passersby from seeing what is inside. While it may be easy to attach posters and other display materials to these backs, it is claimed that people are more likely to enter a store if they can see from the outside that the interior is attractive and comfortable. For this reason, some business owners prefer open-backed windows.

It is crucial to remember that attracting customers into the store is the first step towards making sales. Furthermore, although people may initially be drawn to one product or type of product, they may ultimately purchase different items. The key is to ensure that customers do make purchases.

Window displays are not the only method of enticing customers into the store. However, they are a relatively low-cost and simple way of doing so, and they should be used effectively whenever possible.

Internal Displays

Effective displays of items inside shops, stores, and showrooms are just as important as window displays. A person who is encouraged to enter a shop by an attractive window display will quickly be put off if the interior of the shop is dirty, untidy, badly laid out, or badly lit. It's crucial to ensure that the items for sale are clean and easily accessible, rather than all jumbled together.

The same applies to the items in a window display. For example, if a person has entered the shop to look at an item that caught their attention in the window display, a sale would be lost if they were told that it was not available. It's important to make sure that the sales staff can easily reach the item that the customer wants, without having to take apart the entire window display.

The goods displayed inside the shop do not necessarily have to be the same as those displayed in its windows, as long as the window display items are readily available to show to customers. The layout of the retail sales premises may vary depending on its shape, size, and items for sale, but cleanliness, tidiness, and accessibility are always important.

In such cases, it's important to have information materials (leaflets or brochures) readily available and easily accessible. A designated area for these information materials (leaflets or brochures) should be created, and it should be properly organized to make it easy for customers to find what they are looking for. It's also important to ensure that the information materials (leaflets or brochures) are up-to-date and visually appealing, as this can leave a positive impression on the customer and encourage them to take further action.

Safety Consideration

When it comes to displays inside a store, it is important to consider safety. Unlike window displays, items inside the store can be touched or handled by potential customers, which could lead to the goods being disturbed, made dirty, or even completely ruined.

For instance, a pyramid display of cans of orange juice with colorful labels may look very appealing, but a child could accidentally knock it over or try to remove a can, causing the entire display to collapse. This could not only cause harm to the child but also result in cans bursting and creating a terrible mess. Therefore, careful consideration is necessary before constructing internal displays.

Security

Ensuring security against theft, shoplifting or pilfering can limit the display of various items inside shops. Valuable items such as Omega wristwatches need to be kept in locked showcases or counters. Although attractive displays can be created, customers should not be allowed to touch or handle these items without the supervision of sales personnel.

In cases where items are sold in pairs or sets, it may be necessary for safety reasons to display or allow customers to handle only one item, such as one shoe from a pair. In such displays, a variety of different sizes, styles, and colors of shoes can still be showcased, but only one from each pair. Alternatively, items may need to be fastened by chains or other means so that customers can handle them but cannot remove them unless assisted by sales personnel.

Insurance

Every human being, every business, and every item - whether living or not - which has a monetary value, faces various risks. These risks may include: -

- The risk of a person being injured in or by a motor vehicle.

- The risk of a business premises or any of its contents such as money, furniture, machines, equipment, or stock being damaged or destroyed by fire.

- The risk of farm animals being injured or killed.

- The risk of money, machines, equipment, motor vehicles, stock, or some other valuable item being stolen.

- The risk of injury due to an accident at work.

Insurance companies provide insurance to individuals and businesses, although in some countries, insurance is provided by state-run organizations. Insurance is all about managing risks, with the purpose of reducing or eliminating the adverse effects of risks or fears arising from risks.

Fortunately, not every person or business suffers the reality of the risks they face. For example, most business people insure their business premises and stocks of goods against losses they would suffer if the premises or stocks were destroyed by fire. However, relatively few businesses actually experience such a disaster. The point is that it's impossible to predict in advance which businesses will suffer financial loss due to fire and which will not.

Insurance companies - called **insurers** - collect premiums from businesses that need protection against losses from, say, fire. The premiums collected are pooled so that there is a fund of money. If a business suffers the disaster of fire, it is compensated or reimbursed financially from the fund. Insurance premiums paid by a business to insure its possessions are an expense like any other it must pay.

Indemnity

In insurance, the person or business who buys the policy is referred to as the policyholder. The primary purpose of insurance is to compensate the policyholder for any loss or damage that may occur due to the insured risk. The aim is to restore the policyholder to the same financial position they were in before the loss or damage happened. This is called indemnity.

Indemnity can take the form of:

- *A payment of money equivalent to the value of the lost or damaged item(s).*
- *The replacement of the lost or damaged item(s).*
- *Repair of the damaged item(s).*
- *Payment of medical and other expenses resulting from an injury or accident.*
- *Restoration, such as rebuilding a building destroyed by fire.*

Insurance Coverage Needed

When it comes to protecting your business, having the right insurance coverage is crucial. Unexpected events and accidents can happen at any time, and without the proper insurance, your business could be left vulnerable to financial losses. That's why it's important to understand the different types of insurance coverages that your business may need.

One of the most common types of insurance that businesses should have is **general liability insurance**. This type of insurance provides coverage for bodily injury, property damage, and personal injury claims that may arise from your business operations. It protects your business against lawsuits and helps cover the costs associated with legal defense.

Another important insurance coverage for businesses is **property insurance**. This type of insurance protects your business property, such as buildings, equipment, and inventory, from damage or loss caused by fire, theft, vandalism, or natural disasters. It provides financial compensation to help cover the cost of repairs or replacement.

In addition to these core coverages, there are several other types of insurance that businesses may need based on their specific industry or operations. For example, **professional liability insurance**, also known as errors and omissions insurance, provides coverage for professional negligence claims and is often required for certain professions like doctors, lawyers, and architects.

Workers' compensation insurance is another essential coverage for businesses that have employees. It provides benefits to workers who are injured or become ill as a result of their job. This coverage helps cover medical expenses, lost wages, and rehabilitation costs, and also protects businesses from being sued by employees for work-related injuries. Other types of insurance coverages that businesses may consider include **cyber liability insurance** to protect against data breaches and cyber-attacks, **commercial auto insurance** to cover vehicles used for business purposes, and **product liability insurance** to protect against claims related to defective products.

Determining the specific insurance coverages needed for your business can be complex, so it's recommended to consult with an insurance professional who specializes in commercial insurance. They can help assess your business's unique risks and recommend the appropriate insurance policies to protect your business and its assets.

Remember, investing in the right insurance coverage now can save your business from significant financial losses in the future.

Uninsured Risks

Uninsured risks in business are potential threats or hazards that are not covered by insurance policies. While insurance is a crucial tool for mitigating financial risks, there are certain risks that are not typically covered by standard policies. These uninsured risks can pose significant challenges to businesses and may result in substantial financial losses if not properly addressed.

One of the most common uninsured risks in business is ***reputational damage. Negative publicity, customer complaints, or social media*** backlash can severely impact a company's reputation and brand image. This can lead to a loss of customers, decreased sales, and ultimately, a decline in revenue. Since reputation damage is difficult to quantify and predict, it is often not covered by insurance policies. However, businesses can minimize this risk by implementing strong public relations strategies, maintaining transparent communication channels with stakeholders, and proactively addressing any potential reputation threats.

Another uninsured risk that businesses face is **cyber security breaches**. With the increasing reliance on technology and digital infrastructure, the risk of cyber-attacks and data breaches has become a significant concern for organizations. While some insurance policies offer limited coverage for cyber risks, many businesses may find themselves exposed to substantial financial losses that are not covered by insurance. To address this risk, businesses should invest in **robust cyber security measures**, including regular updates and patching of systems, employee training on best practices, and data encryption.

Natural disasters and catastrophic events are another category of uninsured risks that can impact businesses. Standard property insurance policies typically cover damages caused by fire, theft, or certain weather-related incidents. However, damages resulting from earthquakes, floods, or pandemics are often excluded or require additional coverage. Businesses should assess the potential impact of such events on their operations and consider purchasing specialized insurance policies or implementing disaster recovery plans to mitigate the financial and operational risks associated with these events.

Legal and regulatory risks are also uninsured risks that businesses need to be aware of. While some liabilities are covered by insurance, businesses may face legal challenges or regulatory fines that are not covered. For example, non-compliance with data protection regulations or violations of anti-trust laws can lead to substantial financial penalties and legal fees. To minimize these risks, businesses should stay updated on relevant regulations, seek legal counsel, and implement robust internal compliance programs.

In conclusion, while insurance provides crucial financial protection for businesses, there are various uninsured risks that require careful attention. Reputational damage, cyber security breaches, natural disasters, and legal and regulatory risks are just a few examples of uninsured risks that businesses should be aware of and actively manage. By implementing appropriate risk management strategies and proactive measures, businesses can mitigate the potential impact of these uninsured risks and safeguard their financial well-being.

Loss of Profits

Insurance against loss of profits is an essential component of a robust risk management strategy for businesses. It provides a financial safety net in the event of unforeseen circumstances or events that lead to a significant decline in revenue or business interruption. This type of insurance coverage protects a company's ability to generate profits and helps mitigate the financial impact of unexpected events.

Loss of profits insurance typically covers a variety of circumstances, such as fire, natural disasters, theft, equipment breakdowns, and other events that can disrupt normal business operations and result in a loss of revenue. It can also provide coverage for business interruption caused by external factors, such as supplier or customer disruptions, government actions, or even pandemics.

To obtain insurance against loss of profits, businesses typically need to provide detailed financial records, including profit and loss statements, balance sheets, and other relevant financial data. Insurance providers will assess the risks associated with the business and determine the appropriate coverage based on factors such as industry, revenue projections, and historical financial performance.

Benefits of having this type of insurance include financial stability during challenging times, protection of the company's reputation, and the ability to quickly recover and resume operations after a significant loss event. It offers peace of mind to business owners and stakeholders, knowing that their financial interests are protected in the event of unforeseen circumstances.

It is essential to work with a trusted insurance provider with experience in providing coverage for loss of profits. A knowledgeable insurance broker can help assess a company's specific needs, determine the appropriate coverage limits, and find the best insurance policy that fits within the company's risk management strategy.

In conclusion, insurance against loss of profits is a valuable tool for businesses to protect their financial interests and ensure continuity in the face of unexpected challenges. It is a proactive approach to risk management that can provide peace of mind and financial stability, allowing businesses to focus on their core operations and long-term growth.

Reducing Risks

Business owners should take action to prevent risks from becoming a reality or to reduce their impact. Some precautions are taken automatically, such as locking doors and windows outside of business hours, turning off electrical appliances at night, and using seat belts in vehicles.

Insurance companies can provide guidance to businesses on ways to prevent risks and reduce the impact of potential losses. This can be achieved by installing fire extinguishers in certain areas of the premises, using better locks and bars or shutters on windows. By following the recommendations of insurers, businesses can reduce their insurance premiums. Insurers can also conduct inspections and surveys of the premises to provide recommendations for increasing safety measures.

Practical Example: F

To conclude this chapter, let's summarize all the various factors we have discussed. Businessman Geoffrey Blair wants to open a bookshop, has enough capital, and registers a company called "Blair Stationers Ltd". He is the largest shareholder and will be the managing director.

Firstly, Geoffrey needs to decide what types of books his shop will sell. Will it offer novels, paperbacks, and inexpensive publications or textbooks, technical publications, and expensive books? Will the business sell new books only, or will it also buy and sell books by wholesaling, retailing, in bulk, by mail-order, or by a combination of them?

Next, he must choose the best location for his shop. If he is going to sell novels and paperbacks, the shop needs to be located in a busy street area where its window displays will attract many passers-by who will buy single copies of books and pay for them at once. But if the shop is going to sell mainly textbooks, it needs to be located near schools, colleges, or a university, but it doesn't have to be in a busy thoroughfare. If the shop is going to sell single copies of books to students, they will probably pay for their purchases at once. But if the business is going to sell in bulk to schools, storage space will be needed to hold large stocks of books. And the business will probably have to allow its customers a period of credit, that is, it will have to sell books without receiving payment for them at once.

Once he has found a suitable place and entered into a long lease with the landlord, Geoffrey will have to:

- Plan the layout of the premises to allocate the correct amount of space for each type of publication for sale.

- Decide on the types and sizes of racks or shelving to be used in the shop to hold the books for sale and how they will be fixed to the walls or otherwise. He also needs to decide what kinds and sizes of display cabinets, counters, etc., will be necessary.

- Decide the layout of the store to hold reserve stocks of books and the types and sizes of racks or shelving to be used. He must plan how new stocks can be supplied to the shop quickly to replace those books sold.

- Decide on the number of staff needed to sell in the bookshop itself, plus any others who might be needed in the store or for reordering books and/or accounts work. Recruit them and, if necessary, train them.

- If books are to be sold wholesale, in bulk, then a delivery van might have to be bought, and a driver might have to be employed.

- Decide what machines and equipment (e.g., computers, cash registers) will be required inside the shop and how much can be spent on them. He must also decide what sales documents might have to be printed.

- Decide on the publishers and/or wholesalers from whom stocks of books will be ordered, as well as on the sizes of the orders.

- Plans will have to be made to stop possible pilfering (stealing or shoplifting), and the necessary precautions taken.

- Decide what advertising/publicity will be undertaken, such as signboards and/or signs on the building or in windows, advertising in local newspapers, circulars to potential customers, etc. He also needs to decide whether to have special paper or plastic bags or wrapping paper printed with the name and address of the shop.

- Decide whether to offer special price reductions (or to use some other form of sales promotion) to attract customers to the new shop quickly.

- Order accessories or consumables, such as adhesive tape, string, pencils, pens, pads, and so on.

Geoffrey will have to make many other plans and decisions once stocks of books actually start arriving and have to be housed in the store or displayed in the shop and its windows. Arrangements for banking and for services, including utilities needed - electricity, telephone, water – will all have to be made well in advance of business startup.

This example is relatively simple, but it provides an overview of what is involved in planning, in this case, in figuring out how to sell books. The planning necessary to set up a factory to produce a range of tinned food products or a motor vehicle will be much more wide-ranging and complex. Such planning can also arise after the establishment of an enterprise. For example, at a later date, it might be decided (by the owner or board of directors) to diversify the bookshop so that, in addition to books, it will also sell or rent video tapes or DVDs. Plans will have to be made on how that will be done, how the new section will operate with, or independently of, the existing organization, and so on.

CHAPTER QUESTIONS FIVE – CHAPTER 5

No.1. Describe some of the factors which will dictate the layout of the premises of a business. What should always be the main objective of the layout selected. (maximum 40 marks)

No.2. (a) Describe two ways in which it might be possible for a business person to buy items of furniture or equipment without having to pay the full price at one time. (maximum 20 marks)

(b) Explain the need for adequate insurance cover to any business, mentioning the risks which might have to be covered. (maximum 20 marks)

No.3. Place a tick in the box against the **one correct** statement in each set.

(a) "Depreciation" refers to:
1.☐ the gradual reduction in the value of working assets over a period of time due to wear and tear.
2.☐ a reduction in the number of customers due to new competition.
3.☐ prices which have to be paid for products after deducting discount.
4.☐ a payment to a shareholder as part of the profit made by a company.

(b) Care must be taken with displays inside a shop or store because:
1.☐ they must contain goods ready for sale to customers.
2.☐ they must match the displays in its windows
3.☐ there is more space available than in its windows.
4.☐ customers can disturb them by touching or knocking against them, or by removing products on display.

(c) If machines are bought on hire purchase (HP):
1.☐ they immediately become the property of the business.
2.☐ they have to be paid for in full at the time of purchase.
3.☐ they do not become the property of the business until the final instalment has been paid.
4.☐ they never become the property of the business.

(d) Electrical work needed in business premises is best done:
1.☐ after moving in so it will be known where sockets, etc., are needed.
2.☐ by the owner or staff to save costs.
3.☐ after any redecoration has been done.
4.☐ before any repainting or the laying of new floor coverings.

(e) Displays of products in shop/store windows:
1.☐ should be changed every day to provide variety.
2.☐ need to be built by professionals called window dressers.
3.☐ must be attractive and appeal to the eyes of passers-by.
4.☐ are only suitable for the sale of goods.

No.4. Place a tick in the box against the one correct statement in each set.
(e) The term working assets refer to:
1.☐ the owner of a business and any staff employed by it.
2.☐ machines and equipment a business needs to function efficiently.
3.☐ materials and goods needed for production or for sale.
4.☐ the times during which a business is open to attend to customers.

(b) Keys to business premises:
1.☐ must be as few as possible, and be kept safely to avoid losing them.
2.☐ should be in the possession of every person employed by it.
3.☐ should be hung prominently on a hook within easy reach of all.
4.☐ should be hung around its owner's neck for safety.

(c) Passers-by are:

1.☐ people who walk or drive past the business's premises.
2.☐ previous customers who might buy from the business again.
3.☐ large retailers who buy directly from producers and manufacturers.
4.☐ premises which have been found to comply with safety regulations.

(d) With insurance, indemnity is intended to:

1.☐ ensure a business person gains a profit from his or her misfortune.
2.☐ reduce the risks which are insured against.
3.☐ place a policyholder in the same financial position as before a loss.
4.☐ allow a policyholder a reduction in normal premiums.

(e) Public liability insurance is essential to compensate:

1.☐ an employee who suffers injury by an accident at work.
2.☐ a visitor injured whilst on the premises of a business.
3.☐ for the loss of assets due to fire, theft or water damage.
4.☐ for losses of assets due to actions by members of the public.

(2 marks for a statement correctly ticked – maximum 20

Chapter 6
ORDERING AND STORING IN BUSINESS

Introduction

Ordering and storing are crucial processes in business operations. Ordering refers to the task of procuring the necessary materials, products, or services required for the smooth functioning of a business. This includes assessing inventory levels, tracking demand, and contacting suppliers or vendors to place orders.

When it comes to ordering, businesses must establish efficient systems and processes to ensure timely and accurate procurements. This could involve implementing an inventory management system that tracks inventory levels in real-time, automating the order placement process, or establishing relationships with reliable suppliers who can provide competitive pricing and timely deliveries.

On the other hand, storing refers to the storage and management of the ordered items or inventory. Effective storage practices are vital to ensure that products or materials are well-maintained and readily accessible when needed. Depending on the nature of the business, storage can range from warehouses to simple storage rooms or shelves.

In the storage process, businesses need to consider several factors such as space optimization, proper handling and care of goods to prevent damage, implementing security measures to protect valuable items, and employing appropriate inventory management techniques to keep track of stock levels. This may involve implementing a barcode system or utilizing specialized software for inventory management.

Efficient and well-organized ordering and storing processes contribute to streamlined operations, cost-effectiveness, and customer satisfaction. By ensuring prompt order fulfillment and maintaining optimal inventory levels, businesses can meet customer demands in a timely manner, minimize wastage, and avoid costly disruptions in their operations.

In conclusion, ordering and storing are essential functions in business that involve procuring necessary materials or services and managing them efficiently. Implementing effective systems and strategies in these areas can contribute to improved operational efficiency and customer satisfaction.

The type of business being conducted, the size of the premises, the number of employees, the type of customers, and the budget allocated for the furnishing and equipping of the business premises are some of the factors that dictate the needs of the business. It is important for the business owner to carefully consider these factors in order to create a comfortable and functional work environment that can help improve productivity and customer satisfaction.

Wholesaler Businesses: Streamlining Supply Chains for Efficiency and Profitability

Wholesale businesses play a crucial role in the supply chain by connecting manufacturers with retailers, ensuring a smooth flow of goods from production to end-consumers. With their ability to purchase goods in bulk and distribute them to smaller businesses, wholesalers provide essential services that help drive efficiency and profitability in various industries.

One of the primary benefits of engaging with wholesalers is the cost savings they offer. By purchasing goods in large quantities, wholesalers can negotiate lower prices with manufacturers, passing on those savings to their customers. This allows retailers to access products at a more competitive price point, enabling them to remain competitive in their respective markets.

In addition to cost savings, wholesalers also provide a streamlined distribution process. They consolidate products from multiple manufacturers and deliver them to retailers, reducing the number of individual transactions and simplifying the logistics involved in product sourcing. This efficiency not only saves time but also reduces the administrative burden for retailers, enabling them to focus on other core aspects of their business.

Moreover, wholesalers often offer a wide range of products under one roof, serving as a one-stop solution for retailers. This eliminates the need for retailers to source products from multiple suppliers, simplifying their procurement process and ensuring consistent availability of inventory. This convenience and reliability allow retailers to meet the demands of their customers promptly, thus enhancing customer satisfaction and loyalty.

Furthermore, wholesalers play a crucial role in market expansion. They act as intermediaries, providing a platform for manufacturers to reach a broader customer base. By leveraging their extensive network and market knowledge, wholesalers can expose manufacturers' products to retailers who may not have been aware of them or may not have had access to them otherwise. This increased market exposure opens up new avenues for growth and helps manufacturers expand their reach, ultimately leading to increased sales and market share.

To thrive in the competitive wholesaler industry, businesses must focus on building strong relationships with both manufacturers and retailers. By understanding the needs and preferences of manufacturers, wholesalers can negotiate favorable deals and secure a steady supply of high-quality products. Similarly, establishing trust and credibility with retailers is crucial to ensure repeat business and long-term partnerships.

Wholesalers typically look for products that have high turnovers, which means they can be sold quickly in smaller quantities to their retail customers. They usually avoid products that require breaking bulk, or opening large packages and repacking them into smaller ones, as it wastes both time and money.

For instance, when a manufacturer supplies 100 individually packaged items in a single large outer package, but most retail customers only order a dozen or half a dozen at a time, the wholesaler's staff would have to do a lot of unpacking and repackaging work. In such cases, wholesalers would prefer to receive 20 packs of 6 items each in one outer package.

In conclusion, wholesaler businesses play a significant role in streamlining supply chains, driving efficiency, and facilitating profitability in various industries. Through their cost-saving measures, simplified distribution processes, comprehensive product offerings, and market expansion opportunities, wholesalers contribute to the overall success of manufacturers and retailers alike. Embracing a customer-centric approach and fostering strong relationships within the supply chain are key factors to thrive in this industry and achieve sustainable growth.

Retail Business

Retail businesses play a significant role within the global economy. They serve as a crucial link between manufacturers or suppliers and consumers, providing a platform for the exchange of goods and services. Retail businesses can range from small local stores to large multinational chains, and they operate in various sectors such as clothing, electronics, groceries, and many more.

Retail businesses come in a wide variety of sizes and sell a diverse range of products. There are small kiosks, market stalls, corner stores, and village shops selling goods to local communities. Suburban shopping areas have shops of various sizes catering to the needs of the surrounding residential areas. High street town center shops host stores of different sizes and specialties. There are also larger establishments like huge department stores, supermarkets and chains of supermarkets, hypermarkets, shopping centers/malls, DIY centers, garden centers, and so on, providing a wide range of products and services.

The success of a retail business relies heavily on effective merchandising, customer service, and marketing strategies. Retailers must carefully curate their product offerings to meet the demands and preferences of their target market. They need to ensure that their products are attractively displayed and easily accessible to customers. Additionally, excellent customer service is essential for building customer loyalty and driving repeat business.

To stay competitive in the ever-evolving retail industry, businesses need to employ effective marketing techniques to attract and retain customers. This can include advertising through traditional media channels, utilizing social media platforms, and implementing loyalty programs to incentivize repeat purchases. In recent years, online retail has also become an integral part of the industry, with businesses establishing e-commerce websites and utilizing omnichannel strategies to provide a seamless shopping experience across multiple platforms.

Retail businesses also face various challenges, such as increased competition, changing consumer behaviors, and economic fluctuations. Adapting to these challenges requires staying informed about market trends, investing in technology and infrastructure, and fostering a customer-centric culture within the organization.

Most retailers are interested in any **advertising support** they can receive, as well as any **display material** and **sales aids** provided to them. The original appearance and appeal of products and their packaging to consumers is often of paramount importance to retailers. This is especially true for retailers who sell products via self-selection, where customers choose products from shelves or display cases.

To remain competitive in business, wholesalers and retailers must purchase the right **types of products** at the **right prices** and then resell them at a profit within a reasonable time frame. They need to continuously turn over their stocks and money as quickly as possible. Stocks and money are referred to as *circulating assets.*

In conclusion, retail businesses play a fundamental role in the economy and require careful management and strategic planning to thrive in a competitive and ever-changing landscape. By understanding their target market, providing exceptional customer service, and employing effective marketing strategies, retail businesses can position themselves for success in the industry.

Groups of Wholesalers and Retailers

The competition from large-scale retailers has taken a toll on many wholesalers and small retailers. However, some retailers have found ways to survive by offering specialist or personal services. While many small businesses have been forced to shut down, others have managed to stay afloat by forming groups. In these groups, wholesalers combine their orders to manufacturers and producers, which increases the size of their orders and attracts larger discounts - resulting in reduced prices.

Retailers in the group place most of their orders with the wholesale group. In return, they benefit from the lower prices paid by the group. Some wholesale groups also offer assistance with advertising and promotion under the group name, as well as guidance on layout and design of premises, increasing efficiency, and managing stock ranges and levels - all while making a profit.

Buying or Purchasing

We have emphasized that purchasing high-quality materials at the right time and price is crucial to selling products quickly and at a profit.

Orders and Ordering

When a business needs materials and goods, they purchase them from **suppliers.** The act of requesting products from a supplier is called **ordering**, and it is also referred to as **placing an order**.

Oral **orders** can be risky because they may be misheard or misunderstood, resulting in the **wrong** products being delivered. This can lead to problems like loss of production or sales.

Therefore, it's always best to put orders in writing to avoid any disputes in the future. Orders can be delivered to suppliers through hand delivery, mail, email, or fax.

Finding Suppliers

When starting a business, it is important to find reliable suppliers for the materials and goods you need. If you already have experience in your industry, you may already know who the best suppliers are. However, if you're new to the industry, there are several ways to find potential suppliers. One option is to contact a chamber of commerce or trade association in your country. Another option is to look for trade magazines or journals related to your industry. You can also check the yellow pages in telephone directories or look for advertisements in local or national newspapers. If you have access to the internet, you can do a search to find potential suppliers. If you require products from another country, you may need to import them. In this case, you can contact the trade sections of the Embassies or High Commissions of the countries you're interested in. They can help you connect with businesses that want to export products to your country.

Catalogues and Price Lists

Suppliers often publish printed catalogues that describe their products. These catalogues can be large or small booklets and may contain the prices of the products, as well as any discounts and credit terms offered. Alternatively, the prices, discounts, and credit terms might be listed in a separate document. It's recommended that you obtain catalogues and/or price lists from at least two competing suppliers. This allows you to compare their prices, discounts, and credit terms before deciding which supplier(s) to order from.

Quotations and Estimates

When you require specific products of a certain quality and quantity, you may need to request suppliers to provide a quote in advance for their prices, discounts, and credit terms. Suppliers usually provide this information in the form of a quotation, which is a specially typed or printed document. In some cases, the products you require may need to be specially obtained or manufactured, or there may be work that needs to be done such as painting, decorating, or building. In such cases, suppliers or tradesmen will need to estimate their costs on materials and labor. This process is often referred to as costing, and they will provide you with an estimate in the form of a specially typed or printed document (see Fig. 1/1).

Fig. 1/1   Letter giving an estimates for work to be performed

---

ZONTAL ENTERPRISES LTD
QUALITY WORK ASSURED AND FULLY INSURED

23 SMITH AVENUE, LONDON RN54 LM13
TEL: 321564. MOBILE 789765400

23 November 2023

Dear Mr. Jonah,

Thank you for the opportunity to assess the work required at 17 Emmanuel Avenue. Our quotation for performing the necessary work is as follows: -

We will prime and paint all skirting boards, doors, and door surrounds in eggshell white.

- The materials required for the job (paint, wallpaper, etc.) will cost US$500.00.

- We estimate the labor required to be 48 hours at a rate of US$15 per hour, for a total cost of US$600.00.

The total cost for the job will be US$1,100.00. If you approve of this estimate, we can begin the work during the week commencing 3 December.

Please do not hesitate to contact me or Ssonko Dauda if you have any further questions or concerns.

Thank you again for considering our services. We look forward to hearing back from you soon.

Yours sincerely,

Ashley Dauda
Associate

Always obtain multiple quotes from suppliers or tradesmen to compare prices.

Choosing Suppliers

When choosing a supplier, price is often the main consideration. However, before placing an order, there are other factors to consider. **These include:**

1. Proven Quality from a Known Supplier

It is always better to pay a little more for products that you know are of acceptable quality, rather than paying a lower price for something that is of inferior quality. You can request samples or specimens to examine before placing an order.

2. Reliability of Delivery

It is important to **know** that a supplier can fill and deliver orders quickly, or can be relied upon to deliver them on the promised dates. This helps in planning orders. Knowing that a supplier can deliver quickly might mean you can place smaller orders, which will reduce the amount of money you have tied up in stock and the storage space required.

3. Forming an Association with a Supplier

It might be worth paying a little more to a supplier who values your business. They are likely to give priority to your orders and to satisfy you in other ways. This advantage may not be available with a new, unknown supplier who may make promises to gain your order but cannot keep them.

4. Discounts and Credit Terms Offered

Discounts are reductions offered from normal or list prices of products. They may reduce the prices charged by a particular supplier below the prices charged by other suppliers. Discounts are usually shown as a **percentage**, e.g. 5%, 10%, or 15%. There are two major types of discounts that might be offered to your **business: -**

Trade discount: This is offered to customers who purchase materials or products often in bulk or large quantities either:

> **a.** *With the intention of **reselling** them to their own customers.*
> *or*
> **b.** *for use in the **manufacture** of items that will eventually be sold.*

Quality discount: Discounts and credit terms are common incentives offered by vendors to their customers. A quality discount is a discount offered to customers who purchase products in large quantities, encouraging them to buy more than they normally would. Such discounts might be offered on a sliding scale, with the percentage of discount increasing as the quantity bought increases.

Credit refers to the ability of a customer to purchase products without paying for them immediately. Rather, the payment can be made at a **later date.** The time between the purchase date and the due date of payment is known as the ***period of credit.*** The period of credit can vary depending on the vendor's eagerness to make a sale and the reliability of the buying business in paying its debts on time. It could range from 7 days to 90 days or more.

In some cases, businesses might need to pay a higher price to gain a longer period of credit, particularly when they have a cash-flow problem. When it comes to **consumer goods**, two other factors to consider are well-known brands and advertising.

Well-known brands are likely to offer guarantees or warranties to ensure customer satisfaction, as they have their reputations to protect.

Advertising and Publicity: Goods that are **well advertised** are likely to sell faster, even if they cost slightly more than similar goods. It's important to note that your business might also need to offer discounts and credit terms to customers to persuade them to buy from you. We'll discuss this in more detail later.

In addition to discounts and credit terms, you might also need to print and issue catalogues and price lists. Depending on your business type, you might also need to provide potential customers with quotations or estimates.

Once you've identified your suppliers, it's important to decide how much and when to order. You'll need to forecast the likely demand from customers and the supply of the products you'll make and/or sell.

In an established business, keeping records of usage or sales can be a great help in making future orders. Additionally, maintaining stock records that indicate the quantity received, the quantity used or sold, and the **balance** of each item can be useful.

If you have experience in the same line of business, it is easier to estimate your needs. However, if you are new to the business, you will have to make an educated guess. Ordering too little can result in lost production or sales, as small orders may not be as efficient as larger ones. Furthermore, placing many small orders can be more time-consuming and costly than placing a single large order.

On the other hand, placing orders that are too large can tie up money in stock that could be used elsewhere. Additionally, larger stocks require more storage space. It is crucial to achieve a balance between the *two factors*:

1. *holding sufficient stock to maintain continuous and uninterrupted operations, and*
2. *avoiding tying up money unnecessarily in stock.*

The closer the balance, the more profitable the business is likely to be.

Practical Example: G

Adam Leigh, the owner of a footwear shop, needs to plan and forecast his inventory in advance to ensure that he has the right products available for his customers.

He knows that certain types of footwear are in demand at specific times of the year. For instance, in the summer, customers are likely to buy lightweight, open-toed shoes and sandals, while in the winter, they prefer heavier, closed shoes and boots. Therefore, Adam must order different types of footwear from manufacturers or wholesalers in advance, considering the expected demand for each type of shoe.

He cannot simply order any footwear without proper planning. He needs to forecast the quantity, size, color, and style of each type of shoe that his shop is likely to sell in the upcoming season. Adam's experience in the business helps him make accurate predictions about the types and sizes of footwear that are popular year after year.

As the fashion industry is constantly evolving, Adam must keep up with the latest trends and styles, especially when it comes to women's footwear. This means he needs to **research the market** regularly, as well as reading trade magazines and manufacturers' catalogues. These resources can provide valuable insights into what colors, styles, and types of footwear are likely to be popular in the near future. Additionally, Adam should pay attention to the types of footwear that are heavily advertised, as this is an indicator of increased demand. By staying up-to-date with the latest trends and fulfilling customer demand, Adam can ensure he doesn't lose sales to his competitors.

It's important to consider other factors when deciding on the pricing strategy for footwear. For example, if the economic conditions in the country or region where the shop is located are not favorable, it may be better to stock moderately priced products rather than expensive ones. Additionally, competition is a crucial factor to consider. If a rival footwear shop nearby has recently closed down, it's likely that sales will increase. However, if a new footwear outlet has opened up nearby, it's likely that sales will decrease.

Order Forms

The documents used for placing orders are commonly referred to as **order forms.** Order forms used by different businesses can vary greatly in terms of shape, size, design, wording, and color. Order forms can be completed either by writing, typing, or by computer printer.

Regardless of the mode of completion, an order form must always provide **sufficient information** to ensure that: -

> *The **correct** supplies are received at the right time, and at the agreed prices, discounts, credit terms, etc.*

The information given to the prospective supplier is accurate and free of errors. A mistake on an order form can lead to the delivery of too few or too many items or the wrong products in terms of type, size, color, or quality. In such cases, the supplier might not be responsible for the error and may not agree to accept the wrong products back or replace them with the correct ones. This can lead to problems for you and cause production and/or sales loss.

It is essential to ensure accuracy and completeness when filling out an order form to guarantee that the right products are delivered at the right price and within the agreed time frame. Moreover, keeping a copy of each completed order form is necessary to maintain a record of the stock that has been ordered, when the date, and from whom.

An order form should contain the following information: -

- ❖ The name and address of the ordering business, including contact details such as telephone/fax number and email address.
- ❖ The name and address of the supplier.

- ❖ The order reference or serial number.

- ❖ The date of the order.

- ❖ A detailed description of each item, including size, color, quality, exact quantity required, and the agreed price. Often, the supplier's catalogue or reference number is stated to help identify the term precisely.

- ❖ Any discounts offered.

- ❖ The required delivery date.

- ❖ The method of delivery, such as "by air," "by rail," or "to be collected."

- ❖ Any special instructions, such as "urgent" or "mark fragile."

The signature of an authorized person, such as the owner or manager of the ordering business, is required to place the order.

Sometimes, instead of an order form, a letter might include full details of the items required or the work to be performed.

Upon receiving an order, the supplier might send the customer a confirmation of order or an acknowledgment of order. This confirms that the order has been received and will be filled. Furthermore, it might state the estimated delivery date. This is called **feedback**, and it is essential to know whether an order you have placed can be filled. If not, you can place the order with another supplier.

It is crucial to follow up with suppliers to ensure that deliveries are fulfilled on time. If a **consignment** (a supply of items) is late, it could cause problems or sabotage your business. Finally, once the consignment is ready, the supplier might send the customer an advice note as an advance warning. There might be times when items ordered might be collected from a supplier in your vehicle.

Fig 1/2. A specimen order form

HERBAL WELLNESS STORES			
Helm Logistics Lane, West Sussex. Tel: 1273 442345 Email: info@herbal			

ORDER

No.0974

Date:………………

To
……………………………….
……………………………….
………………………….
Please supply the following items on the terms and conditions agreed

Catalogue Number	Description	Quantity	Price

Method of delivery…………………………….. Delivery date……………
Discount:…………………………………………… Credit terms:…………..
Special instructions………………………….. Signed…………………….

Receiving Deliveries

When you receive a shipment from a supplier, you will normally be given a delivery note (also called a consignment note), which lists the details of the items included in the shipment. This includes the description of each item, its catalogue number (if applicable), and the quantity of each item being delivered. The note will also indicate the total number of cartons or packages that make up the shipment.

The first step you should take when you receive a delivery is to check the delivery note against the order you placed. The descriptions and quantities listed on both documents should match. If there are any discrepancies, you need to take note of them.

Next, inspect the delivery closely. Count the number of cartons or packages to confirm that they match the number listed on the delivery note. If possible,

❖ *count or weigh the number of each item to verify that the correct quantity has been delivered.*

❖ *check the items to ensure that they are the right size, color, and quality.*

❖ *finally, check for any signs of damage.*

If the shipment is large, you may not be able to inspect every item in it. In such cases, you can perform spot checks on a few packages to ensure the contents are correct.

It is important to note that the person receiving the consignment is required to sign the delivery note as proof of delivery. The most common issues with incoming shipments are shortages (less quantity than expected) and damage (which may have occurred during transit). If you notice any shortage or damage, you should write down the details on the delivery note immediately. Failure to do so may result in the supplier or insurer refusing to accept liability.

If the shipment is large or arrives late in the day, you may not be able to inspect it all at once. In such cases, it is advisable to write "received uninspected" or similar wording on the delivery note before signing it. This way, if any issues are discovered later, you can inform the supplier.

Storage of Stock

After inspecting the terms in a consignment and finding them acceptable, it is important to store them safely. Maintaining an inventory of various materials and goods is crucial for almost every business as it is not practical to operate with only one of each item to be sold or used in manufacturing or an office. Therefore, a reserve of frequently used or sold materials and goods is maintained. As items or materials are sold or used, they can be replaced or replenished from the stocks held in reserve.

To illustrate the matter, let's take the example of Adam Leigh footwear shop.

The shop displays a variety of shoes, boots, and other footwear both in its windows and inside the shop. It is inconvenient and time-consuming for Adam and his assistants to remove footwear from the display each time a customer wants to try a pair. Moreover, for security reasons, only one size and color of each style or type of shoe, boot, sandal, etc. is displayed at any given time.

Instead, when a customer expresses interest in a particular style, the shop assistant would inquire about the size and color preference of the customer. Then they would try to find the right size and color from the pairs of footwear held in reserve. Popular items in the most popular sizes are usually kept inside the shop, on shelves, or in cabinets. But other pairs are kept in a separate stock room, to which Adam or his assistants can go to find the footwear concerned. To ensure that a pair of shoes or other footwear is quickly replaced when sold, another pair should be available in the store or stock room.

No business can operate efficiently if every time a product is sold or used up in manufacturing, it has to order a replacement from the supplier or manufacturer. Though items may run out of stock from time to time, good stock control can reduce or eliminate such happenings. It ensures that replacements are received in good time and are available when required to replace those items sold or used.

Why Stores are Needed

The term 'store' is commonly used to refer to a retail outlet where goods are sold to consumers, such as a general store or a department store, in some countries. However, in this context, 'Store' (with a capital 'S') refers to *an area designated for the storage of materials and/or goods required for production, sales, distribution, or safekeeping.*

The items received, housed, and issued by the Store are collectively known as stock. Proper stock control is of utmost importance because the value of the stock is often greater than all other assets combined in a business. Stores are crucial in many ways.

For instance: -

❖ Retail shops, like the Adam Leigh Footwear Shop, require Stores to hold stock for sale to customers and to replenish sold items.

❖ Wholesalers use Stores to hold goods purchased in large quantities from manufacturers until they are required in smaller quantities by retailers.

❖ Manufacturing companies, such as footwear factories, must hold stock of all components used in making different products, e.g., leather, plastic, heels, buckets, nails, and glue.

❖ Offices require stocks of essential items like paper, envelopes, pins, clips, computer consumables, etc.

❖ Even businesses that provide services, like garages, require stock of spare parts for vehicles, consumables like oil, and tools for mechanics' use.

Stores can be quite small, like a stock cupboard in a travel agency or small office, or massive like stockyards for businesses that must have vast stocks of different items available for efficient operation. Many businesses have stores of varying sizes between these two extremes.

Costs of Storage

Maintaining stocks can be costly for businesses. The expenses incurred by a business that maintains stocks can be classified as follows (although not each classification might apply to every business): -

❖ Interest on capital tied up in the value of stocks held. This can be looked at from **two aspects:**

❖ **(a)** if a business has surplus money, that money can be invested to earn interest. But by using some or all of that money to purchase stocks, the income which could have been earned is lost to the business.

(b) In many cases, stocks purchased have to be paid for before they can be used or sold in their original forms or after processing to produce income for the business. In order to finance the purchase of stocks pending receipt of the proceeds of the sale or use of them, a business might have to operate on borrowed money, perhaps in the form of a bank overdraft, and interest is payable on the money so borrowed.

❖ The cost of providing suitable storage facilities, including building or renting and maintaining suitable and secure premises, and, where necessary, providing suitable environmental conditions needed if stocks are not to deteriorate (for example, heating, cooling, semi-refrigeration, etc.), and the cost of storage equipment.

❖ Materials handling expenses, which include wages of stores personnel, and the cost of purchasing, maintaining, and running often expensive materials handling equipment.

❖ General stores operating expenses, such as heating, lighting, rates, cleaning, depreciation, repairs, and many more.

❖ Administration expenses, including the salaries of managerial, supervisory, and clerical stores staff, the maintaining of stock records, the documentation of receipts into and issues from the stores, and the general expenses of running the stores office.

❖ Losses due to the spoilage of stock, theft, pilfering, fraud, etc., and from stock becoming obsolete.

❖ Insurance cover, which is essential if the business is to be able to replace any stocks lost in the event of fire, theft, flood, etc. Insurance premiums to compensate for such losses are expensive, as are premiums for cover to provide compensation for injury suffered by people working in or visiting the stores.

Location of Stores

The locations, sizes, designs, and layouts of store buildings vary from business to business. Factors that can cause differences include the size of different businesses,

❖ the types, ranges, and complexities of their activities, and

❖ the volumes, ranges, sizes, and types of items to be stored.

A store is best located close to the section of the business it serves the most, such as the factory area or the sales area, to reduce the movement of items. In general, the best location for a store is likely to be on the ground level. There are several advantages to locating a store on the ground level as opposed to an upper storey of a building, *including:-*

- **Minimized problems with weight:** If a store is located on an upper storey of a building, there is a danger of overloading, which means placing more weight on a floor than it was designed or built to carry.

- **Eliminated risks of damage and accidents:** Items will not have to be moved (perhaps carried) upwards and downwards by stairs, lifts, escalators, etc., as they would if the store was located on an upper storey of a building. This will save time and labor and reduce the risks of damage and accidents happening while moving items upwards and downwards.

- **Smooth receipts and issues:** Receipts into and issues out of the store should be made more smoothly.

However, these advantages might be outweighed by other priorities or considerations. For instance, the ground floor of most commercial buildings is usually the most expensive to rent and is the most sought after for both production and sales use. Therefore, depending on circumstances, the store of a business might have to be located on an upper storey.

Stores Doorways and other Openings

When planning doorways and other openings for stores, it is important to consider several *factors:-*

Firstly, **security** is crucial and all doorways and openings should be lockable to prevent theft.

Secondly, they should be positioned in a way that allows for a smooth and uninterrupted flow of items in and out of the store.

The number of doorways and openings should be kept to a minimum to maintain a smooth flow and reduce security risks.

Additionally, **the size** of the doorways and openings should be large enough to allow easy access for all vehicles and handling equipment like forklifts.

All doors should be easily kept open while items are being moved and should be able to close and lock quickly. Depending on the situation, standard size hinged doors or sliding doors may be used.

In some cases, normal hinges can be replaced by springs to automatically close the doors after they have been opened. It's important to note that too many doorways or openings may limit the freedom of arranging shelves and racks along the walls.

Stores Floors

Floors are one of the most important parts of any store, as they have to support the weight of the items held in the store, as well as the shelves, racks, etc, in which or on which they are housed. Floors must also provide a flat surface for wheeled equipment, whether it is manually or power operated.

Therefore, floors must be hard-wearing, hard, and smooth. When possible, they should also have slip-proof and dust-proof surfaces. Concrete floors are the best option, but where that cannot be used (e.g. on upper storeys of old buildings), wood blocks or planks are alternatives, provided they are in good condition.

Heating/Cooling in Stores

There is often a need for temperature control for materials and goods stored. Some items need to be kept in refrigerated cold or frozen conditions, while others need to be kept in warm, dry conditions.

Additionally, for the comfort of staff entering or working in the store, in some countries, a degree of heating (which might differ from one time of year to another) is needed. Stores in some countries might also need cooling, at least at some times of the year.

Stores Layout

The layout of stores greatly varies depending on the size and shape of a particular store, its location, access/exit points, the types, quantities, and sizes of the items housed in it, and the activities of the business.

Economy: Usually, storage space is limited, and it must not be wasted. Therefore, the most commercial and efficient use must be made of the maximum area of storage space available.

Accessibility: The Store must be organized in a way that makes it easy to locate and retrieve items with minimal time and effort.

Flexibility: It should be flexible and adaptable to accommodate changes in the inventory and business operations.

Protection: The layout should prioritize the safety of both the items and the people working or visiting the Store.

Movement: Additionally, it should minimize the distance that items and people need to travel within the Store, especially for staff moving items manually.

Equipment for Stores

A wide range of equipment is available to store the huge variety of items that might be housed in Stores. The type of equipment used in a particular Store will depend on several factors, *such as:*

-the size, layout, and location of the Store;

-the variety of different items handled;
-the nature of the items stored: their sizes, shapes, bulk, weight,
properties, and special storage needs;
-the containers/packaging, if any, in which items are packed.

The main types of equipment used in Stores can be grouped into two categories:-

1. Equipment designed for the **storage** of items, such as shelves, racks, bins, cupboards, and trays.

2. Equipment used to **move items**, such as trolleys, pallet trucks, and forklifts.

3. Shelving is the most common type of **storage equipment** used in Stores.

Shelving in a particular Store might need to be of different lengths, widths, and heights to hold different items. In some cases, shelving is made of wood, but metal shelving is usually preferred.

Slotted-angle metal shelving is very popular. It is relatively cheap and lightweight. It is quick and easy to assemble, so the owner or staff of a business can usually do it themselves. The upright lengths of metal have holes bored in them at regular intervals along their entire length, and there are also holes bored in the ends of the shelves. Bolts of the correct size (usually supplied together with the upright lengths and shelves) are inserted through the holes in the uprights, at the required distances apart, and through the holes in the ends of the shelves. The nuts are then tightened on the bolts.

Such shelving can either be fixed to walls or can be freestanding. A length of the shelves, usually 3 meters, 4.5 meters, or 6 meters, can be bolted to another **bay** to form a **run.** The number of bays in a run can be as many as space and requirements dictate, and the distances between shelves in different adjoining bays can differ.

The distance between shelves can be adjusted fairly easily when items to be stored change. Because there are many holes in the uprights, even the shelves in one day can be fitted at different distances apart. Such shelving can be used to considerable heights (say 4 to 41/2 meters), as well as in fairly shallow areas because the uprights can easily be cut to the required lengths.

Fig.1/3. Open Shelving

Cupboards and cabinets are a popular alternative to shelving, especially in smaller stores or when added security is necessary for valuable items or protection from dust and dirt, such as with stationery or clothing.

These storage solutions typically feature lockable doors and adjustable shelves, with the compartments able to be divided into sub-compartments and pigeon holes using dividers. Retaining strips can also be added along the front to prevent items from rolling out or off the shelves if needed.

Fig. 1/4. Hand-operated pallet truck   **Fig. 1/5.** Hand-trolley

Tools and machines used for the transportation of goods come in different shapes and sizes, with both manual and powered options available. Some of the most commonly used equipment includes trucks, forklifts, conveyors, and cranes. While some of these require manual operation, others are powered for greater efficiency. Here are a few examples of such equipment.

Fig. 1/6. Lockable metal cupboard   **Fig. 1/7.** Cabinet with
draws

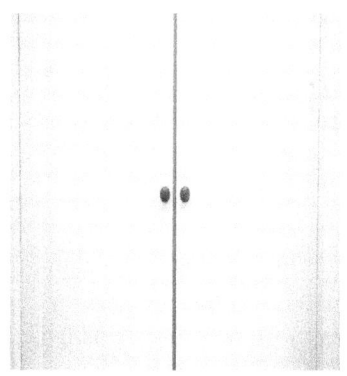

Pallets are custom-made equipment that serves the dual purpose of moving items using fork-lifts as well as storing them. Often, suppliers deliver goods to stores on pallets, which can be easily handled and stored by staff. The same pallets can be used to issue the goods when required.

Fig. 1/8. 2-way entry pallet pallet

Fig. 1/9. Electric forklift for moving

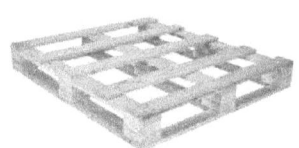

Stock Control

Remember always that depending on the type of your business, its stocks might be one of the most valuable if not the most valuable of all its assets. All stock **must be protected from loss or damage**. Losses of stock can cause harm to your business, and losses of profit. Whatever the size or value of stocks held, it is therefore necessary to exercise managerial control over that stock.

What we refer to as **stock control** or **inventory control** comprises mainly the clerical and administrative functions of store work. It involves:

The following are important aspects of stock management:-

Ensuring that the right types and qualities of items needed for production, sale, and distribution are always available when required.
Protecting stock from various hazards such as theft, pilfering, spoilage, and fire.

Issuing stock in the correct sequence, first in first out, to avoid deterioration of older stock that has been kept too long in the store.

Maintaining accurate manufacturing records that show the movement of items into and out of the store, controlling and monitoring those movements, and keeping full records of the items in the store.

Setting and maintaining the correct stock levels of various items, making reorders in good time, and ensuring that orders are received.

Checking, counting, or measuring stock to ensure that records are accurate and no losses are occurring due to pilfering, theft, damage, or poor storage.

Pricing and valuing the items in the store.

Prevention of Theft

Theft often occurs when unauthorized individuals gain entry to a store by breaking in through doors or windows. To reduce the likelihood of such incidents, the following steps should be taken:

Keep the number of **doorways** into the store to a minimum.

Ensure that **all doors** are strong, fit well, and have adequate locks, bolts, etc.

Ensure that **all windows** and fan lights that can be opened are securely locked. **Wired glass** can help reduce the risk of windows or fan lights being broken to gain entry. Any vulnerable windows, such as those in walls bordering roads, lanes, or waste ground, should be protected by metal bars, mesh, or lockable shutters.

Guard keys closely, as even the best locks are useless if keys are left lying around or are lost. Only a few sets of keys should be available.

Consider fitting **burglar alarms** to doors and/or windows.

Install closed-circuit television (CCTV) cameras at strategic points in the store, as well as at entry and/or exit points.

Prevention of Pilfering

Pilfering refers to stealing by individuals who have been granted access to the Store. Pilferers usually target small items, especially those with some value, like spark plugs for motor vehicles, spanners, and torch cells, which can be easily hidden in pockets and taken out of the Store.

To reduce or eliminate pilfering, the following steps can be taken:

1. **Restrict entry into the Store**: As much as possible, the number of people allowed into a Store should be limited.

2. **Lock away target items**: Items that are or are likely to be attractive to pilferers should be stored in lockable cabinets. More valuable items, such as watches and jewelry, should be kept in safes and strongrooms.

3. **Install closed-circuit television (CCTV) cameras** at strategic points in the Store and at entry and/or exit points.

Protection of Items in the Store

Spoilage of items in a store can occur due to various reasons. Some of the major causes of spoilage include bad handling, water damage and dampness, dirt and dust, incorrect temperature and humidity, contamination, rodents and insects, and incorrect issue order.

Bad Handling: To prevent spoilage due to bad handling, staff should be trained in materials handling and containers holding fragile items should be marked clearly.

Dirt and Dust: Regular cleaning and dusting of storage sections is essential to prevent spoilage due to dirt and dust.

Temperature and Humidity: Temperature and humidity levels must be appropriate for the items being stored. For instance, fruits, vegetables, and cheeses require semi-refrigerated conditions to avoid spoilage, while materials such as plastic and chemicals can deteriorate if temperatures are too high or too low.

Contamination: Contamination is a major concern when it comes to storing certain items. It's important to ensure that items that are likely to cause contamination, such as chemicals or oil drums, are kept well away from foodstuffs to prevent them from becoming contaminated and potentially inedible or poisonous if consumed.

Rodents and insects: Insecticides or traps can be used to eradicate pests, but specialist firms might have to be called in severe cases. Using a first in, first out rule can prevent

Incorrect Issue Order: Incorrect issue order and ensure that older stock is always issued before any stock received more recently, thereby reducing the chances of deterioration.

Fire Protection

To prevent fires and minimize damage and injuries, it's important to take general precautions such as:

❖ **Prohibiting smoking** in and around the store. *"No Smoking"* signs should be prominently displayed at the entrance(s) and inside the store. The rule should be strictly enforced for everyone who enters the store.

❖ Installing an **alarm system** that can quickly alert all personnel in case of a fire outbreak.

❖ Providing **fire-fighting equipment** suited to the items stored in the store. The equipment should be placed at strategic points in the store and in nearby areas. Common fire-fighting equipment includes buckets filled with sand or water, hoses (usually on reels), fire blankets, and fire extinguishers. Fire extinguishers are metal cylinders containing water, foam, or dry powder.

Stock Records

Stock records are an essential part of managing inventory. They are records of information and facts about stocks that are received into or held in and issued from the store. These records can be set down by hand, on a typewriter, or another machine, or in some other permanent form, such as input to a computer, for future reference. The purpose of stock records is to show the quantity of each item in stock at any given time. Without accurate and up-to-date stock records, it would be necessary to physically count or otherwise measure the quantity of an item in stock each time that information was required!

To provide the necessary information, the record for each item must show, in chronological order, the following details:

❖ *the **quantity** of the item **received**,*
❖ *and the **quantity** of the item **issued**.*

The difference between the total number received and the total number issued is called the balance, which is the quantity of the item that should physically be in stock.

Basic Stock Records

Stock records can be as simple or as complex as required. In its simplest form, a stock record might look like the one shown in Figure 1/3. However, a stock record may contain more information about an item, such as its average usage, price, supplier(s), and stock levels set for it.

Fig. 1/10. a simple stock record

ITEM: VITAMINS – B COMPLEX							
Date	Receipts	Issues	Balance	Date	Receipts	Issues	Balance
1-3	500	-	500				
4-3	-	40	460				
9-3	-	400	60				
14-3	300	-	360				
18-3	-	90	270				

Accuracy in Stock Records

It is essential to maintain accuracy in stock records. If a stock record shows an incorrect balance for an item, problems could arise. Two examples illustrate just how vital it is that stock records are maintained accurately.

➢ **Maintaining accurate stock records** is crucial for business operations. Inaccurate records can lead to delays in replenishment orders, causing a shortage of items and resulting in loss of production and sales.

➢ **On the other hand**, if a stock record shows a lower balance than the actual balance, a replenishment order may be placed too early, leading to an excess of items being held in the store and unnecessary financial strain.

Accuracy in stock records is not limited to calculating new balances, but also requires careful attention while making entries from primary documents such as delivery notes, goods received advices, requisitions, and indents.

Stock Levels

Shortages of necessary items can lead to **serious problems** for a business, just as holding **excess stock** can. To avoid such problems, it is important to maintain the **correct** stock level for each item.

❖ Shortages of Stock

A shortage of necessary items can result in loss of production, sales, customers, and profits. To prevent such losses, the store must have the required items in the correct quantities and quality, at the right time.

❖ Excess Stocks

Holding excess stock means that the business's funds are unnecessarily tied up. This can lead to a loss of production, sales, customers, and profits. To avoid such losses, borrowing may be the only option, but this will increase costs through interest payments and reduce profits.

Moreover, occupying space with excess stock not needed for immediate use means smaller quantities of necessary items might have to be ordered. **This can lead:**

> ❖ *to the loss of discounts for bulk buying, and*
> ❖ *frequent small orders can increase costs.*

Furthermore, there is a greater risk of excess stock deteriorating, becoming obsolete, and causing further losses as explained earlier

Setting the Correct Stock Levels

It is crucial to set and maintain the appropriate level for each stock item, neither too high nor too low. Several factors need to be considered while deciding on the stock levels for each item. Some factors are applicable to all items, while others depend on the nature of specific items or materials.

❖ The average usage of an item in production or sales must be taken into account. Larger stocks of important materials and fast-selling items must be held to avoid holdups or interruptions to production or sales.

❖ The usage or sales of an item should be analyzed to determine if they are increasing, reducing, or static. The average usage of an item can be calculated by adding up the quantities issued during a period and dividing the total issued by the number of months. For example, if 225 of an item were issued in January, 300 in February, and 240 in March, the total issued in the quarter was 765. That total divided by 3 gives an average monthly issue of 255.

❖ The time required to order and receive new replenishment supplies is a critical factor. It is necessary to consider the time taken to place orders, find new suppliers, and how long it will take for suppliers to deliver the replenishment stock ordered. Some supplies may be obtainable quickly, but sometimes components and/or finished products have to be specially made or imported from another country, which takes time.

❖ The shelf life of an item must also be considered. Some items, such as fresh foodstuffs, deteriorate quickly, while others last much longer.

❖ A reserve might need to be kept in case of delays in receiving new supplies or for more extensive than usual usage.

❖ The space available in the store, which is usually limited, and how much money the business can afford to have tied up in stock should also be considered.

❖ The price of an item is another significant factor. It is desirable to keep stocks of expensive items to a minimum, so long as the operations of the business do not suffer. However, there might be other matters to consider, such as:-

- *Discounts available for bulk buying.*
- *Seasonal or other price fluctuations.*
- *Expected price increases that might force buying earlier than intended.*

The following stock levels can be set for items:

The minimum stock level (MSL) is the level **below which** the stock of an item should **never be allowed to fall**. Items such as essential raw materials, popular selling lines, important spare parts for machinery, etc., could seriously harm the business if they run out of stock. So, their minimum stock levels should never be reached.

The reorder stock level (RSL) is the level above the MSL at which action must be taken to ensure the order and delivery of new supplies of the item before the MSL is reached.

The higher stock level (HSL) is the level at which the stock of an item should **not be allowed to exceed**. It is set to avoid having capital tied up unnecessarily and the other problems with excess stocks we have explained

Stocktaking and Spot Checks.

Stocktaking is the process of physically counting, weighing or measuring the quantity of each item in stock, and recording the result. It is usually carried out once a year in smaller businesses, typically on the last day of the financial or trading year.

Stocktaking is important because it can reveal losses or discrepancies between stock records and the actual stock. However, because it is only done once a year, spot checks can be used to detect possible losses more frequently.

Spot checks are different from normal stocktaking because;-

- *They are carried out at **irregular intervals** throughout the year.*
- ***Without** prior warning.*
- *Usually involve only a **few random** items.*

Spot checks are designed to discourage storekeeping staff from engaging in malpractices that result in losses, such as pilfering or fraud. By checking items at irregular intervals, staff are less likely to know which items will be checked and when. Another important function of spot checks is to disclose any losses of the items concerned. If irregularities are found, checks can be carried out on a wider range of items without delay. This reduces the likelihood of malpractices occurring between one stocktake and the next.

CHAPTER QUESTIONS SIX – CHAPTER 6

> *Recommended Answers to the Questions-against which you may compare your answers-are in the Appendix after the end of this Chapter. The maximum mark which may be awarded for each Question appears in brackets at the end of the Question.*

No.1. Explain the reasons why businesses have to maintain stocks, and why they need stockrooms or Stores. (maximum 40 marks)

No.2. (a) Describe the difference between the operations of wholesale businesses and retail businesses, and what they seek in products. (maximum 20 marks)

(b) Explain what is meant by placing an order, and the action you would take before placing an order. (maximum 20 marks)

No.3. Place a tick in the box against the **one correct** statement in each set.

(a) Wholesale businesses may be called "middlemen" because.
1.☐ their premises are located in the center of town and cities.
2.☐ in the distribution chain they are the link between manufacturers and producers, and retailers.
3.☐ they are partly manufacturing and partly trading businesses.
4.☐ they deal only with medium-sized quantities of products.

(b) Any trading business:
1.☐ needs to buy the right products at the right prices and resell them quickly at a profit.
2.☐ depends for its success on passing trade.
3.☐ needs attractive window displays in order to attract passers-by to its products.
4.☐ needs delivery vehicles, such as vans and lorries.

(c) An Order Form:
1.☐ gives instructions to staff on how to work efficiently.
2.☐ tells a supplier the sequence in which deliveries are to be made.
3.☐ tells a supplier the descriptions and quantities of products which are required, when and to where.
4.☐ keeps records of stock received and issued.

(d) With regard to a stock item, its balance is:
1.☐ its weight.
2.☐ the quantity of it which has been received by a Store.
3.☐ the quantity of it which has been issued by a Store.
4.☐ the quantity of it actually in stock; total receipts less total issues.

(e) Groups of wholesalers combine their orders:
1.☐ so that retailers will listen to them more obediently.
2.☐ as larger orders attract larger discounts, and lower cost per unit.
3.☐ so that they can increase the prices they charge to retailers.
4.☐ so only one delivery van is needed.

No.4. Place a tick in the box against the one correct statement in each set.

(e) A supplier's quotation:
1.☐ contains descriptions and prices of goods available.
2.☐ is so called because it is given orally, e.g. by telephone.
3.☐ states the price for a specific quantity and quality of products.
4.☐ tells the ordering business that a consignment is on the way.

(b) A confirmation of order by a supplier is helpful because:
1.☐ the ordering business will know whether or not it will be filled.
2.☐ people working in the Store will be alerted to receive the consignment.
3.☐ the order can be placed with another supplier instead.
4.☐ it states what has been delivered in an incoming consignment.

(c) Pilfering is:
1.☐ theft of stock by persons who have been allowed into the Store.
2.☐ theft of stock by persons breaking into the Store.
3.☐ loss of stock due to bad handling, such as being dropped.
4.☐ loss of stock by fire or water damage.

(d) Trade discount is offered to:
1.☐ encourage a customer to buy a large quantity of an item.
2.☐ customers buying items in bulk for resale or to use in manufacture.
3.☐ help customers afford to buy the cost of the products they need.
4.☐ allow customers to buy smaller quantities of products than normal.

(e) Pallets may be used in a Store:
1.☐ to separate storage areas from one another.
2.☐ as guidance in selecting the supplier with whom to place an order.
3.☐ to indicate where items needed can be found in the Store.
4.☐ for moving items into and out of it, and storing them on.

(2 marks for a statement correctly ticked – maximum 20

RECOMMENDED ANSWERS TO SELF ASSESSMENT QUESTIONS 1 TO 6

We give below our generalized answers to Questions in each of the Tests.
✓ If you answered those Questions in a general way:
Compare your Work with our Recommended Answers;

✓ If you answered any or all of the Questions with reference to a specific business (which you run or intend to run):
Use our Recommended Answers to check that you have not overlooked any important matter (s) which could adversely affect that business.

Test One

No.1. Basically, a Business Plan is a guide to the achievement of business objectives. The intention of a Business Plan is to set out in advance, on paper, what a particular business should or will be, what it is intended to do and to achieve, and how it will go about achieving its objectives.The business plan should set out clearly and honesty what the activities of the business will be in order to achieve its objectives; particulars, such as the skills, knowledge and experience, of the people who will run the business and/or work in it, from where the business will operate; what market there is for the products it will make, produce, buy and sell or provide; what competition there is; how much money is needed to start the business, to equip it and get it ready to operate, and how the needed money will be "raised"; and an indication of how much profit the business is expected to gain, year by year, for some years ahead.

A business plan is important to be sure that all relevant matters have been carefully considered before a new venture is "launched". Without a proper Business Plan, matters might be overlooked or not thought enough about. For example, expenses which might have to be paid before the business is started might be under-calculated. A well thought-out business plan gives confidence not only to a new business person, but also to people who might be approached for financial assistance such as a bank manager.

No.2.(a) Put simply, the capital of a business is the money or money's worth invested in it by its owners. Before any business is started some money will be needed to fund it. How small or large the amount needed will be, will depend on the type of business, the size it will be to begin with, and the activities in which it will be involved. The capital needed by, say, a small service-providing business will be quite modest. A small workshop or factory will need more because more will have to be spent on equipping it and getting it ready to operate.

The main types of expenses which might have to be paid before a business is stated are: machinery, furniture and equipment; stocks of materials or goods for resale; payments for rent of premises, legal or professional fees, electricity and telephone; advertising; wages or salaries if employees are needed.

(b) The term is the period over which a bank agrees to provide a loan to a customer. It is counted from the date money is made available by the bank, until the date on which the loan (or the final instalment of it) has to be repaid. The rate of interest is the percentage of a loan which has to be paid in addition to repayment (s) of the loan itself. It is paid to the bank for the right to use the money loaned.

A bank usually requires some form of security or collateral before it will loan money. That might be some possession(s) of value belonging to the borrower, which can be seized and sold to repay any part of the loan not repaid by the borrower.

No.3,The right statement from each of the sets selected and ticked:
a) 3√
b) 4√
c) 1√
d) 2√
e) 2√

No.4,The right statement from each of the sets selected and ticked:
a) 1√
b) 4√
c) 2√
d) 3√
e) 3√

Test Two

No.1. A sole-proprietorship business is owned by just one person, who raises the capital needed. He or she might run the business single-handed, or might have help from family members and/or one or more employees.

A partnership firm is jointly owned by two or more people (called "partners"), working together with the common aim of gaining profits from their business. In general, all the partners contribute to the capital needed by the business, but not necessarily in the same proportions, and each owns a "part of the business, which is called a "firm" or a "practice".

The capital of a limited liability company is divided into shares, which people and/or organizations buy in order to contribute to the capital. They are called shareholders, and they share in any profits made by the business, depending on the number of shares in it each owns.

There are advantages and possible disadvantages to each of the three types of business ownership. Which is right for you depends on your personal and financial circumstances, and the situation in your country, or area of it. If a business is not of the type which will need a large loan, and is unlikely to "run up" substantial debts, the risk of sole-proprietor or a partnership (with a partnership agreement) might be acceptable. However, the advantages of "limited liability" should never by overlooked by any business person.

No.2. (a) The main benefit of securing a franchise for a "territory" is that a business can be established and run profitably without needing large capital investment. Within certain limits (set by the franchiser) the business can be run as an independent unit. The franchisee will be selling a well-known, established "brand" of product(s), which is probably well-advertised. Training and other forms of assistance are usually given by the franchiser, as well as any "leads" in the franchisee's territory.

(b) So long as a person owns or holds more than 50% - more than half – of the issued shares of a limited company, he or she has effective "control" over its management and direction. That is very important, and he or she cannot be removed from the board of directors or be prevented from managing the business as he or she thinks fit – so long as the interests of other shareholders are protected. Each share held usually gives it holder one "vote" at meetings of shareholders. If follows that if a person holds more than half the shares issued at any time, he or she will be able to cast more than half the votes, and so can never be "outvoted".

However, if less than half of the issued shares are held, the person holding the remainder, would have control of the company, should he or she wish to exercise the right. If two or more people held the remainder of the shares, they would have to act together (in "concert") to exert control. They might do that if they were unhappy with the management or directions of the business, or the lack of profits being made, or the way in which money was being spent.

No.3. the right statement from each of the sets selected and ticked:
a) 1 √
b) 1 √
c) 3 √
d) 2 √
e) 3 √

No.4. the right statement from each of the sets selected and ticked:
a) 3 √
b) 1 √
c) 1 √
d) 2 √
e) 2 √

Test Three

No.1. Often the type of business dictates where it should or can be located. For example, a business which depends for its trade on passers-by must be located in a busy thoroughfare-preferably at street level-which many customers pass along every day. Shopping malls or arcades (even on upper storeys) are also suitable for such businesses. But businesses which do not depend upon, or seek, passing trade, can be located in quieter areas, away from main streets (perhaps on upper storeys of buildings). Examples are businesses which provide repair and commercial services, wholesalers, manufacturers, building and timber merchants.

A business usually needs to be located conveniently for the market for its products; that is, for people who are most likely to buy its products, and those who can afford to do so. Much depends on the natures of the products a business is selling, and on the financial status of its likely customers; that is, their demands and preferences. A launderette or laundrymat, for example, would best be located in a high-density residential area in which few people own washing machines. Such a business would not have a good market in a working or office area in which few people actually live.

Customers or clients of some businesses will find them, if they are not too inconveniently situated, and if they are situated in areas in which those people feel "comfortable". Other businesses, for example, a vocational college, can be located hundreds or thousands of kilometers from their clients, so long as there are efficient communications (post, telephones, fax, and email.)

No.2. (a) Necessities are basic and staple items which people need. In general, people know what necessity items they need and can afford, and do not need to be persuaded to buy. They will simply ask shop assistants for what they want, or will collect the items from, say, supermarket shelves, and take them to a check-out point where they will pay. Salesmanship is not needed in such circumstances – unless consumers have a choice of similar products, in which case some selling skill might be needed to persuade them to buy one make or brand rather than another.

Luxuries are items which consumers may not really need, but which they can afford to buy, to make their lives more comfortable and enjoyable. There is often a fairly wide range of such nonessential items available, but between which consumers must select, because their spending power is limited. Skillful salesmanship is needed to persuade consumers to spend their money on certain types of products instead of other types, and on specific products instead of on similar ones sold by competitors.

(b) If the location in which a business is established is found from experience to be unsuitable, it might not be easy to move it to another location. Even if that is possible, it will involve expense, and probably loss of customers.

It is therefore important to research possible locations for your business in advance, before making a final selection. A location which seems ideal might, in fact, have hidden problems, which will only be discovered by research. For example, competitors might be planning to move into the area. Or major road works (a bypass for example) might divert traffic (and customers) away from the area. On the other hand, you might learn about factors which can make a particular location more attractive than it seems. For instance, that the local council is offering low rents to encourage new businesses to its area.

No.3. the right statement from each of the sets selected and ticked:
a. 3 √
b. 2 √
c. 1 √
d. 4 √
e. 3 √

No.4. the right statement from each of the sets selected and ticked:
a. 1 √
b. 1 √
c. 2 √
d. 4 √
e. 3 √

Test Four

No.1. A long-established business might be located in a "prime" position. It is likely to have already some or all of the machines, equipment, furniture, materials or goods, needed. It will also probably have a "customer-base" and, if it has been well-run, will have built up customer "goodwill". Although some changes and, perhaps "modernization", might be necessary, purchasing a "going concern" might save a great deal of expense and work in starting up an entirely new business.

Sometimes, if the business "for sale" is in the same line as the business already owned, the one being bought might be made into a "branch".

Another reason for buying a "going concern" might be that its present owner(s) is prepared to buy the business already operating from those premises. The going concern might be "closed down" to "make way" for the new one to be started in those premises.

No.2. (a) Nobody wants to pay more than need be paid for any product and that applies to buying a business, too! At the same time, the present owner(s) of a business will want to receive as much money as they can for that business. They might not want to "disclose" information which could reduce its value, and therefore the sum they will receive for it.

The owner of a business might not deliberately tell untruth, but might simply not mention certain facts. For example, that a large employer in the area is greatly reducing its workforce that is shutting down an assembly line, or is moving to another area, in either case "local" businesses could be harmed. Another example is that a supermarket or shopping mall might be planned for construction in the area.

It is therefore vital you find out exactly why a business is being offered for sale. Once you know that, you can decide whether or not its prospects for future profits are good, or whether it is too risky to buy that business. Also, you can decide whether the "asking price" is reasonable or not.

(b) First you need to know exactly "what" area or amount of usable space is really covered by the lease. You need to know for how long the lease will run (its term) or has left to run (if you are taking over a lease), and whether it can be renewed for a further period; if so, for how long and on what condition? You must know the amount of rent to be paid, and how often payments are to be made (e.g. weekly, monthly, quarterly).

It is important to watch out for any "hidden extra" which you might have to pay in addition to the agreed rent. For example, local council rates, insurance and/or redecoration of the building. You also need to check whether, during the term of the lease, there will be rent reviews or revisions – which invariably increase the rent. If so, on what will they be based, and how often – at what frequency – will they be made.

Make sure, if you are taking over a lease, that the landlord will agree to your doing so. Also, check that the landlord's consent "will not be unreasonably withheld" should you want to move from the premises, or sublet part of them, during the term of the lease.

No.3. the right statement from each of the sets selected and ticked:
a. 2 √
b. 4 √
c. 1 √
d. 2 √
e. 1 √

No.4. the right statement from each of the sets selected and ticked:
a. 2 √
b. 1 √
c. 3 √
d. 4 √
e. 3 √

Test Five

No.1. The major objective of the layout of the premises of any business should be to permit its operations to be performed in the most efficient manner. People in the premises should be able to work efficiently and comfortably, in a safe environment. Visitors also need to be comfortable and safe from injury.

The best layout of a business premises will depend to a great extent on its size and on its activities, or range of activities – what the premises are used for. Different activities by the same business might need differently laid-out sections of the same premises; e.g. a production area and a sales area, as well as different amounts of space for those activities. Also, whether the business will receive many or just a few visitors (customers, clients, deliverymen, etc) might dictate the most suitable layout of it.

The physical conditions of premises will also have a bearing on their layout for a particular business. For example, the shape and size of the premises, where they are located at ground level, on an upper storey, or on one or more storeys in the same building. Sometimes premises are needed in two or more buildings.

The layout of a business' premises needs to be planned, and if necessary it should be altered from time to time as its needs and activities change.

No.2. (a) If items are rented, leased or hired, they are not, strictly speaking, bought because they do not become the property of the hirer (whether a person or a business). The hirer makes regular payments of an agreed amount for the use of the item(s) detailed in an agreement entered into (with the vendor or a finance company), for as long as the item(s) is required.

(b) Under a hire purchase (HP) agreement, the regular payments made to the vendor or a finance company are partly payment for the item(s) concerned, and partly interest on the agreed value. The first payment required is called a deposit, and once that is paid the hirer has the use of the item(s). As soon as the last of the agreed payments (or installments) has been made, the hirer become the legal owner of the item(s).

No.3. the right statement from each of the sets selected and ticked:

a. 1 √
b. 4 √
c. 3 √
d. 4 √
e. 3 √

No.4. the right statement from each of the sets selected and ticked:
a. 2 √
b. 1 √
c. 1 √
d. 3 √
e. 2 √

Test Six

No.1. It would be very difficult if not possible to operate a business with just one of each of the items it is intended to sell or to use (e.g. in manufacture) and to order a replacement each time an item is sold or used. It is more sensible to hold a reserve stock of each type of item used or sold frequently, so that as an item is sold or used, it can be replaced or replenished from the stock of it held.

The reserve of stock might be quite small, or very large, depending on the size of a business, on its type(s) of activities, and on the range of different items it sells or uses. Often, the value of the items a business has in stock is as great, if not greater, than the values of all its other assets added together! To avoid the loss of any part of such an asset (which could seriously affect or harm the business) stock must be kept safety. They need to be protected from theft and from pilfering, and from damage by fire, water, bad handling and other types of spoilage. The best way to protect stock is to keep it separated from all other activities of the business, and from people who should not have access to it. If stock items are small in quantity or in size, they might be housed in cabinets or cupboards, which should be lockable, especially if the items are available. In other instances, stock of items are kept for safekeeping in a lockable stockroom, or more than one more. Large quantities of stock will need to be kept in large storehouses and/or stockyards.

No.2. (a) Wholesale businesses order goods, materials or components in large quantities (in bulk) from the producers or manufacturers of those products. They then resell the products in smaller quantities, mainly to retail businesses. They do not process or refine products; they simply sell them on in the same form as they buy them, but in smaller quantities.

Wholesalers want products packaged in standard, common quantities, so that they do not have unnecessary unpacking and repackaging work. They prefer well-advertised, fast-selling products.

Retail businesses buy products mainly from wholesalers (although some large retail businesses may buy direct from producers and manufacturers). They deal mainly with consumers, and sell products in small quantities, perhaps even one at a time. Small retailers have limited storage space and limited funds, so they need prompt deliveries of new supplies, well-advertised, quick selling products, plus any sales promotion support available.

(b) The term placing an order means requesting a supplier to supply a stated quantity and quality of a product of a certain description, or requesting that certain agreed work be performed.

The first step is to find the best supplier. If you do not know of any already, sources of information include local trade or government offices, chamber of commerce, trade magazines, newspapers advertisements, and the Internet. With products to be imported, the trade offices of the Embassies or High Commissions of the countries concerned might help, as might the Internet.

Having found possible suppliers for your needs, you can request their catalogues and/or price lists, plus details of trade and/or quantity discounts and credit terms, or ask them to quote for the supply, or estimate their charges to you. You might ask for samples or specimens of products. Compare the qualities, charges, discount and credit terms, promised delivery dates, etc, of each before deciding with which to place an order.

Once you have made that decision, send the supplier a completed order form or a letter giving – clearly and accurately a detailed description of each item (size, weight, shape, quality, color, as appropriate) you require. State the agreed prices, discount(s) and credit terms. You must state the names and addresses of your business, and those of the supplier, and the date of the order.

No.3. the right statement from each of the sets selected and ticked:
a. 2 √
b. 1 √
c. 3 √
d. 4 √
e. 2 √

No.4. the right statement from each of the sets selected and ticked:
a. 3 √
b. 1 √
c. 1 √
d. 2 √
e. 4 √